A PATTERN OF FAITH

A PATTERN OF FAITH

An Exposition of Christian Doctrine

by
GEOFFREY PAUL
Bishop of Hull 1977-1981
Bishop of Bradford 1981-1983

with an Introductory Memoir
by
Rowan Williams

CHURCHMAN PUBLISHING
1986

A PATTERN OF FAITH
by GEOFFREY PAUL

was first published by
Churchman Publishing Limited
117 Broomfield Avenue
Worthing
West Sussex BN14 7SF
in 1986

Represented in
Paris, Sydney, Wellington
and Winnipeg

ISBN 1 85093 037 6

Distributed to the book trade by
Bailey Bros. & Swinfen Limited
Warner House
Wear Bay Road
Folkestone
Kent CT19 6PH

Printed in Great Britain by
Whitstable Litho Limited
Whitstable, Kent

CONTENTS

a) The Hull Lectures

b) Sermons and Addresses

Introductory Memoir
by
Rowan Williams

Geoffrey John Paul (1921 – 1983)

In the early summer of 1979, a very well-known and well-loved teacher in the Cambridge Divinity Faculty, Henry Hart of Queens' College, retired from his duties in College and University. A number of those who had been his pupils over a period of more than thirty years met at a dinner to mark this event — something of the end of an era for theology at Cambridge; and among those whom Henry Hart had specially asked to be included in this occasion was an early student of his whose remarkable abilities he still spoke of with warmth and respect. He was not the only one of Geoffrey's teachers to remember him with this degree of vividness. That dinner was the first time I met Geoffrey in person, though his name was already familiar. We talked with some animation; but I had not expected to see very much more of him (the paths of suffragan bishops and junior clergy in theological colleges don't automatically cross all that often). About eighteen months later, though, I met Henry Hart once again, who enquired almost at once whether I had any recent news of that exceptional man, Geoffrey Paul; and I was able to say that I was about to join that exceptional man's exceptional family as his son-in-law.

This memoir, then, is written out of the experience of a brief but deep friendship, for which I am more thankful than I can easily say: Geoffrey was one of the greatest Christians I have ever been privileged to know. Other people can write, and have written, out of longer and fuller acquaintance, and there is every possibility that a full-scale biography will be available before too long. But I hope this brief record will convey something of the man as he seemed to those closest of all to him as a private person — his wife and children, and their families in turn — as well as something of the leader and teacher. He was not only a scholar and a bishop of unusual stature, but a man who commanded love and loyalty in a rare degree, from the most diverse souls. That too is to be remembered and celebrated.

Geoffrey was a Londoner by birth, though commonly agreed in his last years to have made a very satisfactory Northerner by adoption. The second of three children, he enjoyed a specially close relationship with the mother who died while he was still a student. She had done much to encourage and support him in his intellectual development, first at Rutlish School, Merton, then at Queens' College, Cambridge, where he arrived in 1939 with a scholarship. His studies — Modern Languages first, then Theology, with first-class honours in both — were interrupted by war service. He was not without misgivings about this: but it was clear to him (and remained so all his life) that he could not be an unconditional pacifist, and that, given this impossibility, he could not properly shirk the responsibilities of a citizen in wartime. In the event, he served with — predictable — distinction: his linguistic gifts were fully employed in his work as a Royal Navy liaison officer in various French ships under British operational command. In practice this involved an unusual measure of authority and responsibility; he returned to Cambridge much tested and matured.

His sights were now firmly set on ordination, and he was determined to equip himself as fully as possible for the job of an expositor of Christian theology. In 1946, after taking Part II of the Cambridge Theological Tripos, he moved on to King's College, London, where he was able to combine training for the ministry with further work towards the degree of Master of Theology. The time at King's was enormously important in a number of ways. Geoffrey's spiritual life was moulded further in depth and discipline by Eric Abott, then Dean of King's, who imparted the same gifts to so many Kingsmen over the ten years of his pastorate there. Many friendships grew up through King's College connections — with Eric James and John Townroe among others; and a friendship that blossomed into something more began in these years with Pamela Watts, then reading English at King's. She and Geoffrey were to be married in 1951.

Pam recalls an occasion when Eric Abbott asked her, 'Aren't you terrified by his intellect?' There is no doubt that, at KCL, Geoffrey appeared to both teachers and contemporaries as a thoroughly formidable personality, unworldly, intense, apparently destined for an academic career. Professor Peter King of the University of Hull, a friend from childhood days, recalled when presenting Geoffrey for an honorary doctorate at Hull in 1982 the impression Geoffrey made on him and his parents in the 1940s: Professor King saw Geoffrey as possessing, throughout his life, a 'Franciscan' aura, dedicated and absorbed, generous with time and possessions where the disadvantaged were concerned, careless of his appearance and dignity; his mother, in the time-honoured manner of mothers, expressed amazement, having met the student Geoffrey, that the Church of England should ever consider ordaining someone so dishevelled. It was a period in which Geoffrey worked hard at building up a library, sometimes being faced with the classic 'poor student's' choice of a meal or a book — not, for him, a very difficult decision, it must be said. All in all, he was an austere figure to most people: his intelligence could be crushing to the less mentally nimble, and he did not suffer fools gladly. KCL often seemed to him a much more amateurish milieu than Cambridge, as far as religious and theological reflection went, and the fact that he made no secret of this on occasions reinforced the intimidating effect of his presence.

Not surprisingly, a good many of those who knew him found it hard to see him as a parish priest, and assumed that he would be back in Cambridge before long. He did indeed spend only a short time in parochial ministry; but he left it, not for academic comforts, but for the mission field. And the two years (1948-50) he spent at Little Ilford in the Chelmsford diocese were more than a duty to be endured. He rose to the considerable challenge of transmitting what he had learned, and rose to it with enthusiasm — if with only partial success: this was only a beginning in the long apprenticeship of saying profound things simply which bore such astonishing fruit in his last years. He was also uncomfortably forthright on non-theological issues at times, capable of denouncing from the pulpit the notion that a Christian could be a political Conservative. In later life he was less outspoken; but his deep commitment to the ideals of those early years of the Welfare State never weakened.

In 1950, already engaged to Pam, he left for India, under the auspices of CMS. Although he was first sent to a Tamil-speaking area (as chaplain to St. John's College, Palayamcottai), he was detailed to learn Malayalam, to the puzzlement of himself and some of his colleagues; the reason became apparent when it was revealed that Leslie Brown, the Principal of the Kerala United Theological Seminary at Kannamoola, near Trivandrum, had been appointed Archbishop of Uganda. Geoffrey was to join the staff at Kannamoola, with the expectation that he would eventually take over as Principal.

He and Pam were married in Colombo in 1951, and in 1952 they moved to Kannamoola; it was to be their home for thirteen more years. All five of their daughters were born there, and it was more completely home for them than almost any other place in Geoffrey's ministry. He became more and more fluent in Malayalam, teaching and preaching in the language, and his influence was felt well beyond the compound of KUTS. There were contacts with religious leaders of other faiths, with Christian medical students at the hospital in Trivandrum, with the first generation of leaders in the new Church of South India. But the centre of all Geoffrey's work in these years remained Kannamoola, where he trained a very large proportion of the CSI clergy now working in Kerala, including the present Principal (and several of the staff) of KUTS. Among his colleagues was the present Moderator of the CSI. When my wife and I visited Kerala in 1981, we found that the name of Geoffrey Paul was an instant passport to the hearts of church people there, still a vivid and treasured memory.

Once again, Geoffrey had the task of adjusting his teaching to the level of those with very different skills and attainments from his own. Many of his books had to be abandoned when he sailed for India (many others still bear the unmistakeable marks of life in the tropics, the ravages of heat, damp and insects); and he must have recognized during his time at Kannamoola that he had effectively turned his back on original research of the kind he might have done in Britain. But he worked hard at helping to produce the kind of reputable and serious, yet accessible and straightforward, theological literature that was most urgently needed in India. He published in the 'Christian Student's Library' two commentaries on Mark and on John; these — especially the John commentary — are models of condensed and lucid exposition, solidly grounded in the scholarship of the 40s and 50s, and skilfully relating exegetical issues to the questions of the educated Indian Christian and the missionary. In the commentary on John it is clear at several points that he has in mind Westcott's prophecy that we must wait for an Asian to give us the really authoritative reading of this gospel, and hopes that his work may help to enable such a response. He also ventured the speculation that the 'beloved disciple' was John Mark, and that part of the purpose of the gospel was to defend Mark's gospel and its theology; this is ingeniously argued from a novel reading of John 21, but the case has not generally carried conviction among New Testament scholars. The strength of the commentary is in its forceful simplicity of language, veiling a profound erudition and speaking of long and prayerful meditation. Published in 1965, it is a foretaste of the Geoffrey so many knew as a teacher in his greatest maturity, at Lee Abbey and as a bishop.

There were attempts to lure him back to Britain in these years, to theological college work, to Deanships in Cambridge colleges; he gave serious consideration to at least one such approach; but at the end of the day he was confident that India was the station to which he had been called.

Neither then nor at any time did he show the least sign of regret at what a more ambitious man might have seen as lost opportunities. He had the simple and rather rare gift of 'being where he was', of a complete but undemonstrative commitment to the task given him. There were great trials, however, during the time in India. When his first child was still a baby, Geoffrey contracted polio, and had to return to England for treatment, for a period of several months. Happily the only long-term effect of this was a noticeable but not too serious limp. Far more distressing was the crisis that eventually helped to bring the family back to Britain for good. Geoffrey and Pam's fourth daughter was diagnosed as having a form of leukaemia, and there was virtually no chance of appropriate long term medical care being available in India; so, after fifteen years, they prepared to move. In the event, all trace of the disease vanished, within a short time of their return: Geoffrey and Pam ascribed this total and utterly unexpected remission to the prayers of Christians all over South India from the time the child's illness was first known.

This great wave of support in prayer testified with abundant clarity to the love and respect in which Geoffrey — and his family — were held. He had, almost (but not quite) unpredictably, become something of an heroic figure, as well as a father-in-God. It was not only incidents like his rescue of local children from their threatened homes during a heavy flood — though that is something still remembered at Kannamoola, and the subject of a laudatory ode by a local poet! More generally, his stature was recognized as a man of wisdom, insight and sheer intrinsic authority beyond the ordinary. And although he was still capable of uncompromising severity with idle or evasive students, he left no impression in India of the impatience, even arrogance, some had detected in the younger Geoffrey.

The adjustment to England, where the family arrived back in 1965, was not easy. They had, of course, been back more than once on furlough; but most of the children had started school in India, and the whole family was used to the very simple conditions of life at Kannamoola. As so often with the returning missionary, there was an uncomfortable hiatus before a suitable niche could be found. During the year after his return, the family settled briefly in rented accommodation at Southsea, while Geoffrey made what was to be — to his abiding regret — his only return visit to Kerala, invited by the CSI to help in the settlement of one of the sharp internal disputes which have disturbed the life of that Church so frequently. The invitation witnesses to the confidence reposed in him by Indian church leaders: he was one of the few people who could bring both sympathy and detachment to a delicate situation.

In 1966, Oliver Tomkins, Bishop of Bristol — a great bishop with a special flair for picking his staff — invited Geoffrey to become a Canon at Bristol Cathedral and Director of Ordinands, with responsibility also for post-ordination training. The five years that followed were among the happiest in the family's memory. Geoffrey was blessed with a string of exceptionally gifted, imaginative and responsive ordinands and young clergy — people like Paul Bates, Doug Constable, Andrew Louth, Trevor Williams. Here he could engage in teaching and counselling at a level appropriate to his own capacity, stimulating and being stimulated. Oliver Tomkins was a continuous source of support and inspiration, and Geoffrey's colleagues on the Chapter (among them Douglas Harrison, the Dean, and Evan Pilkington) became lasting friends. The Pilkingtons especially were close companions. Geoffrey's sermons were still hard going for the average listener, but he was a sensitive and accessible pastor to very many in the Cathedral congregation and beyond. For all the Pauls, Bristol retained a very special hold on their affections; and the clergy Geoffrey had helped to train were to keep in constant touch with him for the rest of his life, turning to him in crises, relying on his unfailing prayer for them and understanding of them.

The period in Bristol was important in assuring Geoffrey and the family that England and the Church of England really could welcome them again, after the desperate anxieties of the last year in India and the uncertainty and strangeness of the first year of their homecoming. Geoffrey was beginning to be seen as an obvious candidate for a bishopric. Typically, though, he refused to be jostled by other people's expectations: he was never seduced by the lure of the obvious. So when, in 1971, he accepted the appointment of Warden at Lee Abbey, some of his friends and colleagues were rather baffled. It represented, at best, a 'sideways move'; and, rightly or wrongly, Lee Abbey was seen as a place with a strongly and explicitly Evangelical ethos, while Geoffrey was a notably unpartisan man, who had been brought up in a moderate Catholic ambience, and served his title in a church of similar colouring, then trained and worked alongside CMS workers of a rather different background without any sense of strain. Lee Abbey was a surprising place for him to go — or so some thought.

Geoffrey did not think so. He could not take seriously the 'sideways move' argument, being supremely indifferent to the notion of a career. And Lee Abbey stood for priorities that mattered intensely to him — Christian community life, lay education and evangelism. Churchmanship did not matter. The opportunity of guiding and planning the life of a substantial residential community (about seventy people) devoted to the exploration of the faith in new ways, providing an environment in which both the committed and the uncommitted could find a challenge — this was a God-given opening for Geoffrey. At Lee Abbey he came to be better known to more people than ever before. In Bristol he had been a point of orientation for the younger clergy, a star to navigate by; at Lee Abbey, he was to fill this role for great numbers of lay people — groups staying for conferences, casual short-term guests, the resident community, and often their families and friends as well. Lee Abbey was not exactly the kind of religious community envisaged by Basil and Benedict, but Geoffrey had all the qualities the great monastic legislators looked for in a superior — the skill at adjusting to the varying needs of individuals, the sense of responsibility to God for those in his care, the willingness to exercise authority for the sake of the whole group.

He learned a lot about being a father-in-God here that he had not learned even in India and in Bristol, and his teaching skills had their greatest testing and polishing. Here at last he did discover a vein of transparent directness in his expounding of his faith, and a flexibility and responsiveness that stayed with him in his teaching as a bishop. The conferences and events organised by the community became more varied, intellectually and imaginatively; and in this, Geoffrey had invaluable help from his assistants — notably Doug Constable, one of his former Bristol charges, who joined him as a chaplain at Lee Abbey, and whose gifts in music and drama were a wonderful enrichment to the community.

Naturally, there were those inside and outside the community who did not have much sympathy with the new 'feel' of Lee Abbey, and Geoffrey had his share of conflicts to deal with. The Wardenship was a draining job at times. But it says much that he did not suffer from rancour or personal enmity on the part of those he disagreed with — and this despite his willingness to be forthright when he thought it necessary. But all such jobs, 'living over the shop', make heavy demands on families too: the Pauls were conscious of being public property, in a sense, during these years — at a time when the children, now mostly in their teens, sometimes felt the need for more privacy. The family all contributed and were happy in the exceptional beauty of the environment; but all of them, at one point or another, wanted to 'escape' for a while. Holidays came to be very important events — especially holidays at Oliver and Ursula Tomkins' cottage in West Wales, which was to go on being a family refuge throughout Geoffrey's life, a place for which they all felt a special warmth.

The obvious was finally allowed to happen in 1977. Geoffrey's willingness to accept the appointment to a bishopric at this point had a great deal to do with the person from whom the invitation came. Geoffrey recognized something of a kindred spirit in Stuart Blanch, someone who shared his enthusiasm for imaginative evangelism and the equipping of a theologically alert laity. During his four years as Bishop of Hull, one of the things Geoffrey most treasured was his excellent working relationship with Archbishop Blanch and the other suffragans of York. He had always been fortunate in his colleagues, and his experiences at Hull were particularly happy in this respect. At his consecration in York Minster, crowds of friends from Lee Abbey helped to fill the nave; one of them, a brilliant young violinist, had been asked by Geoffrey to play Vaughan Williams' *The Lark Ascending* during the service. Many people were to feel that that poignant and visionary little piece had a peculiar fitness for the ministry ahead.

The family settled happily into a large house at Hessle, a few minutes' walk from the river, and rapidly made friends in the neighbourhood — among them, Alec Horsley, Quaker businessman and benefactor of the Bradford School of Peace Studies. Geoffrey's two eldest daughters married during this time, a third became engaged, one was already making a considerable name for herself as an artist in London, and the youngest won a scholarship at Christ Church, Oxford, in 1980. But the house was seldom empty or undertenanted: apart from family friends and new in-laws, visitors from all previous stages in Geoffrey's career were constantly passing through. There, as later at Bradford, Geoffrey and Pam together exercised a ministry of hospitality which was as important to some people as the more public side of their work. *Their* work; because Pam played far more than a 'background' role, putting great energy and equal sensitivity and warmth into a wide range of activities. Lee Abbey had helped her too to new levels of confidence as a teacher and communicator, and she was increasingly in demand as a speaker.

Geoffrey's episcopate at Hull exceeded even the high expectations so many had had for him. He familiarized himself swiftly with the needs of the area, and his deep and articulate concern about unemployment was an important dimension of his ministry there and at Bradford. What he was — and will be — most remembered for, however, is the triumphant venture which this book commemorates. When the Bible Society, in a survey of religious practice in the UK, designated Humberside a 'Christian blackspot', Geoffrey decided to try and exercise publicly the teaching gifts he had already used so successfully in the more private environment of Lee Abbey. In Lent 1981, he hired the Hull City Hall for a series of weekly addresses on the Christian faith. The planning and prayer that went into these occasions was prolonged: Geoffrey was careful to choose a variety of chairmen for these sessions, to represent a cross-section of the whole community, not just the churches; and he gave a great deal of thought to the kind of environment he wanted at each lecture, using different styles of music to introduce and conclude what he had to say, with the eager help of a number of local groups of musicians. Friends, churches, religious communities, up and down the country, supported him and his helpers with their prayers. Geoffrey was less apprehensive than many others — his anxieties were mostly focused on producing a script of the greatest possible economy and directness. The typescripts have all kinds of tiny emendations easing the flow of exposition, cutting out an allusion that might take too much for granted in his audience, gently underlining a challenge. They are not primarily *literary* compositions but texts for the spoken voice, his own distinctive spoken voice.

Filling a city hall week after week with audiences for lectures on Christian theology is no small task; Geoffrey did just that, speaking to gatherings of up to 1200, and confounding pessimists who had looked with incredulity at the size of the building he calmly proposed to fill. The Hull *Daily Mail*'s columnist, 'Jane Humber', thought the whole course 'something quite unique . . . a clear, yet adult, exposition of the Christian faith. The time, the place, the atmosphere were exactly right'. Geoffrey's obituarist in the *Church Times* rightly said that the Hull lectures became 'something of a legend in the North'. Other bishops followed his example; but the intensity of the experience as presided over by a man of Geoffrey's capacity was hard to reproduce.

By the time the lectures were under way, it was known that he was to move to Bradford in the spring of 1981: the lectures proved to be the climax and consummation of his work at Hull, and the diocese of Bradford became more aware than ever of the kind of man it was getting. Geoffrey was enthroned at the end of April, on a day made memorable by a heavy fall of snow that prevented many fellow bishops and dignitaries reaching Bradford. Local radio announced that the enthronement service would be open to all comers in view of the unexpected number of places thus made available; and the people of Bradford crowded in, packing the Cathedral to the walls. Among those taking part were several representatives of the non-Christian religious bodies in the city: Geoffrey succeeded in returning their greetings in the languages in which they were given — Hebrew, Arabic, Urdu, Gujerati . . .

All the auguries for his new work seemed excellent; and he was once again fortunate in many of his colleagues, like the two archdeacons, Frank Sargeant and David Rogers. But it must be said that he soon felt some of the strain that goes with the more isolated and exposed job of a diocesan, and sometimes missed the 'collegial' atmosphere of the York diocese. He was more often exhausted by his work, though this seldom, if ever, affected his grasp and his efficiency. His episcopal charges, like his powerful enthronement sermon, made it clear that he hoped to make the diocese a body more deeply committed to mission — an authentically 'apostolic' organization, as the Provost of Bradford, Brandon Jackson, was to say in an eloquent memorial tribute, an organization whose structures may be constantly reformed to serve the task of communicating the gospel to an unjust, fragmented and directionless society. There was no doubt that the diocese had a *leader*; there is equally no doubt that, as is the way with *Christian* leaders, it cost him heavily to bear this sort of responsibility.

He instantly inspired real affection, both in the city and in the rest of the diocese. After his death, Pam received moving tributes from lay people in remote farming areas in the Dales who so vividly remembered the Bishop's visit, some small incident, a conversation, a sermon phrase. The same was true of the clergy — and clergy are a notoriously hard group to please. I had the happy opportunity of sharing in the Diocesan Conference at York in 1983, and the trust and warmth between Geoffrey and his clergy was manifest. Many who knew him at this time would have found it hard to believe that he had ever been that rather angular young man who sailed for India in 1950. One of my strongest recollections of him at this time is of his universal generosity of judgment; not that he refused to recognize folly or weakness or empty-headedness, but he was able to accept people, with irony and amusement and real understanding all at once. It was not only in speaking that he had become more direct and simple, there was what I can only call a simplicity in his love for people. Both were rooted in a constantly deepening prayer — something of that 'unifying' of the heart that the great teachers of spirituality have written of. He could still be formidable, he still had all the intellectual and spiritual passion of earlier years — and there is at least one official photograph in which a faint gleam in the eyes suggests that the lion is going to spring if the fussy photographer delays him much longer; but all would have agreed with Frank Sargeant's description of him as above all 'a loving and lovely man'.

His time as a bishop coincided with the raising of a number of different issues in the life of the Church of England and its relations with the state. Geoffrey was not a publicity-seeker, and rather disliked being asked by press or media for 'instant quotes' on public questions; but he reflected hard on many of these questions. The Falklands War of 1982 prompted a judicious comment to his Diocesan Synod, pointing out that Britain had been seen, rightly or wrongly, as showing an embarrassing lack of proportion in its actions, yet wondering whether anything other than some kind of 'police action' by the UK could have satisfied what seemed to be the will of the United Nations; he did not think that there could be any long-term alternative to a negotiated transfer of sovereignty to Argentina. It was a characteristic judgment, devoid of journalistic sloganeering, accepting the legitimacy of limited force, looking hopefully to a future where international agencies could effectively settle such disputes.

In the discussions sparked off by the 1983 report on *The Church and the Bomb*, Geoffrey's feelings were rather divided. He had some sympathy with the idea that Britain might make an independent move in beginning the reduction of nuclear armaments, given the relative unimportance of her nuclear capacity within the Western Alliance as a whole. But he was not an absolute unilateralist; he found the pacifist position untenable (as we have seen) and believed that the nuclear threat had played its part in preserving Europe from another major war. On this issue, his thinking was still developing, and his public utterances on the subject candidly reflected his own explorations and uncertainties. The same might be said of his attitude to women's ordination. He saw no weight in the supposed theological objections advanced by some, but was conscious of the ecumenical difficulties in the background. I do not think it is entirely wishful thinking to suggest that the positive case in favour of the ordination of women to the presbyterate was coming to seem stronger and stronger to him in his last year. Here again, he admitted freely that his views were in the process of formation. He was far less uncertain, though, about the other vexed question of the period, that of the remarriage of divorcees (and especially of divorced clergy). On this, he was a rigorist — though, as might be expected, he was unfailingly respectful of those who had, in conscience, decided and acted otherwise. But he had no doubt that a discipline should be agreed and upheld.

Wider spheres of work opened up in 1982 and 1983. He was appointed in December 1982 to chair the General Synod's Board for Mission and Unity, after the tragically premature death of Bishop David Brown. And the Hull lectures prompted an invitation from the BBC to deliver a slightly shortened version of the course, first on the World Service, then on Radio 4, in the spring of 1983. *A Pattern of Faith* was warmly received by large audiences, and the radio critic of the *The Listener* on March 3 gave enthusiastic commendation to the talks as 'near the top of the table' in religious broadcasting — a rare tribute in a journal that seldom singles out religious items for mention. Versions of the scripts of these broadcasts appeared in the Christian periodical *Third Way*, and there was already some considerable pressure on Geoffrey to publish the whole series as a book; but he was a great perfectionist with the written word, and was reluctant to publish without putting in more work to polish and tighten his text.

The were many new joys in his personal life: the marriage of another daughter, and the birth of a first grandchild were delights within the family; there was an honorary degree from Hull, awarded at the same ceremony as the honorary doctorate of his friend and neighbour, Alec Horsley; there was the deepening friendship with Bishop John Robinson, who was then spending his vacations from Cambridge in the lovely house at Arnecliffe which he and his wife Ruth had bought some time before. Geoffrey rejoiced in the intellectual stimulus John provided for him and for many others in the diocese; and John in turn was delighted to be asked to function as an assistant bishop in the Bradford diocese, helping Geoffrey greatly by performing various duties in the remoter bits of the Dales. The shape and extent of the diocese was always a problem, especially in the absence of a suffragan; Geoffrey and Pam seriously considered taking a caravan on tour to the northern end of the diocese for a few weeks at a time. Geoffrey *and* Pam again: once more, Pam was constantly in demand as a teacher and counsellor, very much a pastor in her own right.

Geoffrey was visibly tired and unwell in the early months of 1983, and by Easter was troubled by oppressive discomfort at the back of his neck and the upper spine. His doctors decided that there was the possibility of a small growth of some kind, and by May it was known that he would be going into hospital for surgery and would be taking a substantial rest from diocesan work. John Robinson agreed to deputize for several matters; but it was in that May that John and his friends learned that he had an inoperable and advanced cancer, and all his plans were radically changed. Meanwhile, Geoffrey prepared himself for hospital, rather looking forward to the chance of doing some solid reading at leisure. He preached the University Sermon in Cambridge late in May and stayed for a few days with my wife and myself, immensely tired but in good, even high spirits. Returning to Bradford, he devoted one sleepless night to composing his own manifesto for the forthcoming election — a fine and forthright piece, not designed to give much comfort to the government of the day, and representing his most mature and considered thoughts on the body politic. He attacked the kind of economics that tolerated mass unemployment, argued for the legitimacy of a deterrent, but urged limited unilateral action by Britain, pressed for improving trading terms for the Third World, and demanded more serious reflection on the implications of the 'new technology'. He also denounced those who invoked the name of God to sanction nostalgia for the 'good old days when all the moral issues were thought to be clearer', and insisted that government 'worthy of the name' must appeal to and live by standards other than 'self-concern and self-improvement'. The Bradford *Telegraph and Argus* featured this manifesto prominently, and ventured an appreciative editorial comment.

The crucial operation, in Leeds General Infirmary, was carried out late in June, and a non-malignant growth was successfully removed; but Geoffrey immediately contracted a post-operative infection which stubbornly resisted treatment with antibiotics. He was in intensive care for nearly three weeks. It is not easy to write anything at all about this time of acute helplessness and anxiety for all those who loved him most. The 'success' of the operation seemed the most gratuitously cruel of ironies. No-one was sure how far he recovered full consciousness — though he recognized and responded to members of the family; and he conveyed a strong sense of acceptance, even content, in these last days. Brothers from the Bradford house of the Community of the Glorious Ascension (to whom Geoffrey was Visitor), and Stephen Humphries, one of the hospital chaplains from Bradford, gave their time and ministry most generously, praying daily with Geoffrey. The diocese joined in deeply felt intercession; the local press and the city followed developments with genuine concern. Those three weeks demonstrated yet again the degree to which the diocese and the local community felt themselves committed in love to a man who had so evidently committed himself to them.

He died on July 10. All those who knew him will still remember the shock and grief at what seemed so meaninglessly untimely an end. Geoffrey's own comments on the pain of meaningless loss will be found in what follows, and their authority is no less than when he first uttered them. You must turn to what he says for a 'reading' of his own death in the light of faith.

He did not specially want to see these talks in print, as we have noted, and the decision to publish was not lightly taken. He was, undoubtedly, a man who set himself unusually high standards for what he wrote; but there are other considerations than literary exactitude. These texts must not be allowed to gather dust, because the most effective Christian preaching is 'the sacrament of a consecrated personality', to borrow the words of a theologian Geoffrey much admired, P. T. Forsyth. What we have here is a profoundly *personal* 'pattern of faith' that communicates precisely because it is in no way an *individualistic* private reflection. It is the vision of someone who is supremely himself because he is more interested in God, Christ, the Spirit, the community of faith, than in his own religious psychology — a central paradox and glory of the life of grace.

His obituary notice ended with the words, 'He was not disobedient to the heavenly vision', an apt text for so very 'Pauline' a man. In his lifetime, Geoffrey Paul drew countless people closer to the challenge and the joy of that vision. I hope and trust that he will continue to do so through his prayers and through these pages.

Jesus Christ, The Way In

My Lord Mayor, I am particularly grateful to you for your presence here tonight and for the generous, friendly and honest things you have said. I think I can say that I do intend over the course of these lectures to refer to most of the matters you raised for consideration.[1] From the first moment when this project began to form in my mind, it was my hope to speak not just to particular groups of people, not just to my own church people or to people of all the Christian churches or even to all religious people of whatever persuasion. I chose the City Hall because I humbly hoped to speak to this city whose name I bear in my title, and of whom I have been a proud and happy citizen these last four years. And whatever you may think of the content of tonight's lecture, I am honoured that the Lord Mayor of Hull has felt it sufficiently part of the Bishop of Hull's job to talk about this Christian Faith in our city to be willing to join me on the platform tonight to open the proceedings.

The aim of this course of lectures is to set forth the Christian Faith as openly, as clearly, as interestingly, as comprehensively, as publicly as I possibly can. For myself, I believe it is God offering himself freely to all men; so that although by my office I am expected to be a guardian of Christian truth, this gospel does not belong to me. God, I trust, is more eager to speak than I am and knows the private language of each one of you better than I do.

I shall try to speak persuasively and with conviction, but it is my hope that you will hear better than I speak, and I hope that you will sense that I am respecting your own right to hear whatever God pleases to say to you.

So, *Christian* faith, in public.

Now let me begin with a quotation from Hans Küng:

'Christian does not mean everything that is true, good, beautiful, human. Who could deny that truth, goodness, beauty and humanity exist also outside Christianity? But

[1] The first of the Bishop's Lectures was delivered on 21st January 1981 in the presence of the Lord Mayor of Hull and many persons from the City and Diocese.

everything can be called Christian which in theory and practice has an explicit reference to Jesus Christ.

'A Christian is not just any human being with genuine conviction, sincere faith and good will. No one can fail to see that genuine conviction, sincere faith and good will exist also outside Christianity. But all those can be called Christians for whom in life and death Jesus Christ is ultimately decisive.

'Christian Church does not mean just any meditation or action group, any community of committed human beings who try to lead a decent life in order to gain salvation. It could never be disputed that commitment, action, meditation, a decent life and salvation can exist also in other groups outside the Church. But any human community, great and small, for whom Jesus Christ is ultimately decisive can be called a Christian Church.

'Christianity does not exist wherever inhumanity is opposed and humanity realised. It is a simple truth that inhumanity is opposed and humanity realised also outside Christianity — among Jews, Muslims, Hindus and Buddhists, among post-Christian humanists and outspoken atheists. But Christianity exists only where the memory of Jesus Christ is activated in theory and practice.'

And that is why these lectures start with Jesus Christ. Rather than talk in generalities, as I might, and try to establish some common ground, I thought it more honest to go straight to the heart of the matter. And yet Jesus, though scandalously particular, is *not* an exclusive figure, but is met with everywhere, often when he is least expected.

Let me quote the story of a young man brought up in an orthodox Hindu family, Sadhu Sundar Singh.

'I shall never forget that day, December 16, 1904, when I burnt the Bible in the fire and my father said: "Why are you doing such a foolish thing?" I said, "The Western religion is false, we must destroy it." So I destroyed the Bible and thought I had done my duty. On the third day I saw the power of the living Christ. That third day I was going to commit suicide because I had no peace in my heart. I woke up in the early morning; it was Winter and I took a cold bath. Then I began to pray, but not to the Christ of Christianity, because I hated Christianity, but I prayed like an atheist for I had lost my faith in God. I said, "If there be a

God, you must show me the way of salvation or I will commit suicide." From 3 to 4.30 early in the morning I was praying. About 5 I was going to commit suicide by placing my head on the railway line, so I had only half an hour more. Then something happened which I never expected; the room was filled with a wonderful light. I saw a glorious figure standing in the room. I thought it was Buddha, Krishna or some other saint whom I used to worship and was quite prepared to worship him, but I was surprised to hear these words: "How long are you going to persecute me? I died for thee, for thee I gave my life." I could not understand, could not speak a single word. And then I saw the scars of the living Christ, whom I thought of as a great man who used to live in Palestine and was now dead; but I found He was living, the Living Christ, not dead and gone . . . When I got up, He had disappeared. I went to tell my father. He could not believe it. "Only the day before yesterday you burnt the Bible. How can it be that you are now a Christian?" Because now I have seen His power . . . It was not a dream. After taking a cold bath nobody can dream. There was reality, the Living Christ.'

Jesus is seen here, not as someone who is, as you might say, shut up inside the Christian Church, but as a more universal figure recognised beyond the bounds of Christendom. And it isn't difficult to find warm appreciative references to Jesus from other Hindus, from Muslims, Jews, Marxists and people of every faith and of none.

A Muslim, M. Hamidullah, in a book review, writes 'Muslims also admit the exalted position of Jesus, who saw with the eyes of God, talked with the tongue of God, and was absorbed in God, a position', he adds, 'which is not incompatible with his not being God, but remaining man, a very exalted man.'

An East-European Marxist, Mikhail Machavu, writes 'But what happened when this man no longer walked through Galilee and Judaea, what began to happen in this man, has, in its range and intensity, no parallel in history. And the names that were given to him have no parallel.'

And, as one of those strange paradoxes, you will never meet a Hindu who will speak other than warmly and appreciatively of Jesus Christ, because of the part Hindus openly recognise the preaching of Jesus' gospel played in the renaissance of their own religion and in the whole movement that resulted in the Independence of India.

Now there is an interesting peculiarity about the way in which Jesus is spoken of here and in the many other references one could list. While they often insist that Jesus should not be thought of as more than a man, again and again he is unconsciously spoken of, not just as one speaks of other great figures of the past, such as Socrates, but as one who has a kind of universality, who is more like a contemporary, who is not tied to one culture but can be thought of as native to anyone anywhere. When people speak of Jesus, it is hard not to feel that they are quite unconsciously speaking of someone who is, as it were, still about, who is not past history, over and done with, but who continually turns up in rock musicals, in visions to people with no Christian background, as a folk hero in liberation movements, as well as in religious revivals in places where to all intents and purposes religion seems quite to have dried up.

These lectures begin with Jesus because, with him, we seem to be talking about someone who is alive, someone who turns up anywhere to remind people of the living God.

And that recalls the basic fact that the Christian faith was first preached only because those who preached it claimed that although Jesus had been put to death quite indisputably, they had in fact seen him again after that death, and knew him to be alive, not only as a ghost or an apparition, but as vitally alive with them and the most important factor of their experience.

Let me say a word or two about the Resurrection. I do not propose to go into detail about the reasons why we claim the Resurrection is historically true — the existence of the Christian church, the change in the bearing of the dispirited disciples, the emergence of Sunday with its special significance, the failure of the new faith's first opponents to produce the body of Jesus; I do not propose to reflect upon the fascinating avenues opened up by the Turin Shroud, more particularly as the results of the latest tests are not yet public. I want quite simply to say that if Jesus had not, somehow or other, come back to his disciples after his death, it is unlikely in the extreme that we should ever have heard of him. Let me take a parallel to illustrate what I mean. I suppose the greatest religious figure of this century is Mahatma Gandhi, who exercised an enormous influence over a wide range of contemporaries, who succeeded in making politics a spiritual thing in a quite new way, who has had a fascination for everyone who has studied him, and who died, something in the manner of Jesus himself, at the hands of his fellow-Hindus for trying to defend Muslims against Hindu violence. In the wake of his death, there were Hindus ready to speak of him as an incarnation of God for this century. Yet it is a sad fact that within a few years of his death the ideals for which he stood and the particular spirit he represented have been abandoned; apart from his aging contemporaries he has left no band of followers, and he has come to be recognised for what he essentially is, one of the very great figures of the past whose teaching and example we can always study and imitate, but who is not in any sense with us now.

Jesus was not as famous in his day as Gandhi. He gets only the merest passing reference in one or two contemporary history-books, there were nothing like the facilities for reporting his activities that existed in Gandhi's day, he could hardly have been thought to be the threat to Roman Imperial power that Gandhi was to British power. Yet Gandhi is past history, a very great man who died. Jesus, too, died in the past, yet he is mysteriously alive to people of every age and race and culture to this very day, and those who worship him do so in every conceivable tongue. There is no other figure in the history of mankind of whom this sort of claim is made, and for whom the claim carries credibility. The Resurrection of Jesus is an extraordinary historical phenomenon that has worked itself into the consciousness of mankind.

Let me now take a step forward.

The Resurrection was the conclusive piece of evidence that persuaded the first disciples that Jesus was more than a man, that he came to them from God and spoke in God's own voice. During his lifetime, they had already become aware that they were in the presence of a quite unique person, but all their perceptions and hopes were dashed when he was ignominiously caught and put to death. The Resurrection was like the awakening after a bad dream, when everything now fell into perspective, when past incidents and remarks now made sense and they saw the picture whole, and astonishingly, for Jews of all people, began to speak of Jesus in ways which are appropriate only of God.

Did they make a mistake?

Did they go beyond the evidence?

Did they, carried away by the enthusiasm of some extraordinary spiritual experience, or intoxicated by the sight of a spiritual movement developing with unexpected success before their eyes, make claims for Jesus that go beyond sober truth, beyond what Jesus ever said of himself?

Did the Christian missionary movement, and that marvellous bogey Saint Paul, in an age of religious credulity, turn the simple Galilean preacher into a divine figure, a Saviour-God beyond anything he ever conceived himself to be?

Is the subsequent Christian faith with all its doctrinal superstructure an ultimately unjustifiable human construct from insufficient evidence?

The Resurrection of Jesus, the sense the disciples had of his livingness with them and the deductions they drew from that experience force us to ask what Jesus actually thought of himself.

To put it baldly, did Jesus think he was God, and did he ever say so?

To examine this question, I must obviously draw on what is written in the gospels, and so it will be necessary first of all to say something about attitudes to scripture. In regard to the claims Jesus made for himself, I shall quote as a rule from the first three gospels which appear to stand nearer to the actual spoken style of Jesus himself than the Gospel of Saint John, which reads more like a devout and penetrating meditation on the life of Jesus for a special clientele. Similarly, I shall prefer not to quote the more obviously dogmatic statements, the great 'I ams' or the names of Christ, which one might perhaps think the first Christians had sharpened and magnified in the light of their later understanding; rather, I shall aim to rely more on those astonishing indirect unconscious assumptions, those passing remarks that emerge from Jesus' ordinary teaching and table-talk, and which, if you tried to remove, you would pull the whole fabric of the gospels to pieces. In other words, you see that I recognise that the gospels are not just tape-recorded, disinterested reproductions of Jesus' uttered words. They are reminiscences preserved by those who revered him and so could have permitted their own enthusiastic worship to colour their testimony. It is right therefore that in reading the New Testament, and indeed the whole Bible, we use the appropriate critical tools and reverent discrimination to see if we can get beyond the writers, as far as possible to Jesus himself. It doesn't take long to discover, of course, that as soon as you try to do so, you bring with you pretty heavy prejudices of your own to the task.

But when we succeed in putting obvious prejudices aside, when we give up deciding in advance what could or couldn't have happened or what must be later exaggeration, we are again and again forced to admit in the light of things Jesus' own followers neither expected nor found easy to digest, and which caused them as much difficulty as it has caused readers ever since, that his biographers have not seriously misrepresented him, and that by and large the gospels give us a trustworthy picture of this extraordinary figure.

Now of this Jesus there are four unusual things the gospels assert.

First, there was his relation to God in prayer.

He taught his followers to pray 'Our Father', a title which was new to them; but he did not, as a matter of fact, line himself up with them and pray 'Our Father', as if he were simply one of them in this respect. He addressed God as Father or My Father or Abba, a term of intimacy and confidence that his contemporaries remembered for its unusualness and which scholarship has recognised to be quite unparalleled in Jewish devotional literature of the time. It is a simple fact of experience that you and I have to be converted in order to pray, and we need some stimulus to persuade us that we can pray in all circumstances, even the worst, to a God who is our unchanging Father. For Jesus, from the very first, prayer was natural, and he prayed to God with an intimacy and a confidence that belonged, as you might say, only to one of the family. His closest disciples recognised that he was at home with God in a way in which neither they nor anyone they had ever met was.

Secondly, there was the way he spoke.

Quite casually, in the course of ordinary conversation, he spoke of himself as greater than the great ones of the past, greater than Solomon, greater than Jonah, greater than David, greater than John the Baptist, than whom none born of woman was greater. He spoke of the generation that witnessed his appearance on the scene as *the* critical, crucial generation to which all other generations led up, the generation for which all history waited in order that accounts might be settled, and he takes it for granted that ultimate judgement will be meted out, not for good or bad behaviour, but for response to him. And oddly enough, unprecedented as these claims sound as I list them here, they do not sound ridiculous or arrogant in the context in which we read them.

Quite unconsciously, he uses Old Testament titles for God, like the Bridegroom, for himself. Quite naturally he assumes that he is the definitive interpreter of the mind of God. 'You have heard that it was said to them of old (— by God, in his law), but I say unto you; for the hardness of your hearts God gave you this command'. He takes it for granted that he has authority to do what the clergy of his day rightly claimed only God can do, namely forgive sins, and demonstrates the truth of his claim by standing a paralysed man on his feet. He foresees that his claims, his movement, his attitude to the church of his day will eventually bring him to his death, but he does not see that death just as an inevitable tragedy, or a hero's death to be borne like a laughing cavalier, or even as the death of a martyr to a cause, but rather as an act foreseen by God, that will ransom mankind, as the sacrifice that will open the way to a new covenant between God and now not just Jews but all men.

Thirdly, a word about Jesus' miracles.

Now some people will no doubt have difficulties about the whole notion of miracle, and we are of course at liberty to scrutinize every miracle-story to see whether it might perhaps have grown in the telling from an ordinary incident with a straightforward explanation into a more impressive account, and we can also take note of the fact that with our scientific upbringing, we are less ready, maybe, than our ancestors to expect miraculous happenings. But when we have exercised the greatest, perhaps even more than necessary, caution, it seems impossible to deny that the most vivid popular impression Jesus made upon his contemporaries was of a man who did wonderful things for ordinary people in the name and power of God. Now miracle stories are told of other great men, and Jesus himself told his disciples that they would do greater things than he, so miracles do not in themselves prove uniqueness, far less divinity. But there is a style about the miracles of Jesus that goes very strikingly with the other sorts of evidence that we have looked at so far. There are none done to show off, none done in response to demands that he should authenticate himself, none done to escape from difficult situations or from the embarrassments of manhood — all features of popular miracle-stories. His miracles seem to be done, in response to human need, to restore situations of sickness, abnormality, hunger, fear to true normality. The assumption behind the miracles, as with Jesus' prayer, is that he is walking in his Father's world where evil, sickness and fear are essentially foreigners and intruders. His miracles are a re-establishing of God's sovereignty in his own world, a banishing of evil from a position usurped, a restoring of things to rights. The miracles are but one more astonishing example of a man who simply cannot view any aspect of human life from any other point of view but God's — a point of view which comes naturally to him.

Fourthly, there is a fulfilledness, a total deployment of all his powers in Jesus that it would be hard to parallel.

Viewed from the *negative* side, this is often called sinlessness. Now of course, you can't prove a negative or demonstrate sinlessness, but it is certainly true that there are no moral accusations, no bits of gossip levelled against him that ever had the least chance of sticking — his trial brought that out. On the contrary, he makes absolutely uncompromising moral demands without ever a footnote or a qualification arising out of some remembered failure or some shadow of a stained conscience; he seems to show no need ever to protect himself against insinuations or slanderous interpretations of his behaviour, no fear of a finger pointed or of some journalist's damning file opened to cause him to rush to the microphone with repudiations or laboured explanations.

Moreover, we have no instance of Jesus amending what he said, apologising, expressing regret or asking pardon for any word or action. And while, in anyone else we can think of, such an attitude would be quite intolerable bumptiousness and arrogance, in Jesus it is so natural that we hardly notice it.

Unconsciously we confess that in his case, word and life make one seamless, unstained robe. Viewed from the *positive* side, here is a short life, much of it spent in obscure waiting for the word Go from God, yet that time not evidently wasted, but spent in gathering all his powers for his brief, meteoric ministry. And in that ministry, with, of course, its choices and renunciations, such a total fulfilment of all his attractive capacities and talents in the undivided service of God that anyone who met him found himself face to face with the ultimate, saw the meaning of his life and the key to its living, was confronted with final judgement and salvation then and there. And in that ministry, such a total obedience to God and all his goodness with no faltering, no losing of his way down by-paths, that it called out all the powers of evil to meet this intolerable challenge, that he finally forced the High Priest, the head of the splendid but too safely-settled church of his day, to ask the one question above all that he had been wriggling to avoid, 'Do you think you are our Messiah, God's very Son. Are you claiming that this is the high-noon, climactic point of history?' — to which Jesus replied without evasion, 'I am'. And because such a breath-taking claim was too much for even a religious leader to tolerate, the High Priest sent him to Pilate to get rid of him. A totally undeviating life with no part of his powers not fully engaged, pointed at every moment unswervingly in the direction of God and his will, revealing with devastating clarity what manhood looks like when God does it among us — Is there any other life remotely like it?

When Jesus' first followers found themselves incredibly in his presence again after his terrible death and then his astonishing resurrection, and when they began to put together that experience with all the remembered experiences of his life with them that we have just looked at, they found themselves driven to two convictions — first, that they would never again be able to visualise God except through his eyes, and then, more frighteningly yet more marvellously, that this man who had been the sharer of their hopes and joys and failings and recoveries, this man who had warmed their hearts and made them see the worst and the best human life is capable of in ways they had never before conceived, could have been none other than God himself walking among them as a man.

Christian faith is founded on the inescapable conclusion that those who had lived closest to him drew, and which is open to be tested in experience by anyone, anywhere and at any time. It is not a later complicated, theological theory, corrupting the simple message of a wandering guru concerned only for human goodness, and invented by the intellectual Saint Paul. It is not a dogmatic system devised by philosophically minded early Greek Christians. It is not an adaptation to the needs of the day, or to currents of thought about virgin-born saviour-gods that happened to be in the air.

The Christian faith that Jesus has opened the way to God for men in a unique, new, full, free and final fashion by living God's own life here among us arose out of his first, ordinary, hard-headed followers' response to the things that happened in their midst. And after the resurrection, they did what no man ought to do in regard to another, what certainly no Jew would ever have thought of doing in regard to another. They knelt down and worshipped him and called him Lord, because they could do no other.

The evidence for Jesus' divinity, particularly all this indirect evidence, is much stronger than is commonly believed.

But before we leave the gospels, along with this overwhelming conclusion that Jesus was to be worshipped, there are two other matters that need to be taken into account.

First, the title Christ. I suppose it has now become a surname, but it is, of course, a Greek translation of the Jewish title, meaning God's anointed Messiah. Now it isn't absolutely clear from the gospels whether Jesus ever actually claimed to be the Messiah; certainly he wasn't the sort of Messiah people had been led to think of, and Jews today still find it difficult to recognise him as the Messiah of their expectations; but in the end, whether he himself used the title or not, his followers found it the only name that adequately described the role he fulfilled. And because Jesus could only be described as God's Messiah, that tells us something very important about the nature of the God whom he came to represent. Jesus was not just a wandering holy man, like an Indian guru, unconcerned for the affairs of the world; he was not like a Greek sage, teaching the perennial philosophy and uninfluenced by historical circumstances; he was not a clergyman or the constituted head of an official religious body — though he isn't exactly a foreigner to any of these pictures. The title Messiah implies that he was the leader of a religious movement, or rather that Israel, whose religion he fulfilled, was itself a movement in world history on behalf of mankind. The title Messiah implies a dynamic. And in Jesus' case his movement began not as the official programme of a General Synod, but as a popular liberation movement with its roots among the poor — and yet what a paradoxical one. It has some of the features that make Jesus the natural hero for other political liberation movements, yet it is hard to find one directly political saying in all his teaching. It was a movement of sufficient public strength and credibility to alarm the authorities, and the triumphal entry is perhaps a more formal title for what we today would call a demo — a march on the capital. Yet Jesus could under no circumstances be called a revolutionary, and while frightening the life out of the authorities, was ready to accept their unjust verdict upon him rather than treat them as enemies to be overthrown by force. His words were firebrands, and he had the power to inspire others to fall in behind him, but his weapons — which in the end lost him all his followers — were complete trust in God at the cost of everything he stood for, and complete love for men, calling no man a fool, hating none, separating himself from none.

And he was willing to give his life for these principles, content to believe that if he was obedient to the end, he would leave God free to do the perfect work that God alone could do. The title Messiah shows Jesus representing a very dynamic God, who seems to work in time and in the toils of history to set men free from whatever enslaves them, free to become a new family of men and women committed, through him, to faith in God and universal love for others. To follow this Jesus will inevitably lead to being involved in some way or other in the course of public life, yet paradoxically, to making an utterly spiritual thing of it, to making it, indeed, one's spiritual life.

And secondly, manhood.

Now it may seem odd to labour the question of manhood when his companions will have known him as a man long before they ever began to have other thoughts about him. But it is in fact true that once you begin to think of Jesus as divine, it is easy enough to forget the reality of his manhood, which is so evidently displayed in the gospels.

His humanity there has the splendid vigour of human powers fully extended, with all the limitations that go with a person born at a particular place and time. His constant journeys suggest a strong physical frame, but, although we never hear of his being ill, we see him worn out, weary, hungry and thirsty. He has all the emotional capacity for friendship and glad human relationships that make him good company at a wedding, a welcome guest in all sorts of houses, trusted by children and at ease among women, some of whom were familiar with the worst side of men. He is attracted to particular people, impressed or tickled by others for their faith, their smart answers, their sincerity; he is angry with others, indignant with his own disciples, heartbroken or amazed by the difficulty some had in trusting God. He had a lively mind and a fresh imagination, readily observing all that went on around him and able to turn it into vivid parables; a quick mind in controversy that not only avoided falling into the traps set for him, that not only could get the better of an argument, but that could also, in his answers, touch the very conscience of his questioners; and his last week in Jerusalem shows a mind able to plan ahead in order to avoid arrest before he has completed his work with his disciples, able in his trials to avoid useless bickerings and force the High Priest in the end to ask the one question he wanted to avoid and that Jesus had come to Jerusalem to put. Yet this mind was not schooled in any institution of higher learning, he was ignorant of many of the things you and I have known since childhood, he had never travelled overseas and spoke none of the languages you and I speak. He was indeed a first century Jew of a particular appearance, height, tone of voice and colour of eyes, with a particular quality and limitation of mind, a particular range of knowledge and of subjects for conversation — Jesus is not just man in general, he was a man. And there are two other limitations to his manhood that both identify him totally with us and at the same time seem to distinguish him utterly from us.

First, he *needed*, like us, to pray, turning aside at all the crisis points to ask his father for guidance, experiencing prayer sometimes as joy, sometimes, as in Gethsemane, as a weary agony of indecision, sometimes, as in the terrible cry on the cross, as a blank wall of silence. Yet although he prays with the same sort of human apparatus as we do and knows he simply cannot get on without prayer, there is nevertheless, as we have seen, a naturalness to his praying that was an astonishment to his contemporaries and remains an astonishment to all who try to follow him. And secondly, in Gethsemane he uttered that unconscious but quite extraordinary exclamation, "Not my will but Thine", making it clear that he didn't have a sort of automatic divine decision-maker inside him, yet taking it for granted, as which of us can ever think of doing, that he can in prayer, fully will the will of God because he has never so far deviated from it. The ultimately astonishing thing about the manhood of Jesus is that, while at every point at which the gospels allow us to test — and they are many — we see a human being endowed just as we are endowed, in him there is no aspect of being a man that falls outside this unique relation with God his Father.

We recognise here a true man, the true man, and it is clear from him that there is no being a man that is not at the same time living in total, confident trust in God: indeed the only suggestion we ever have that he found being a man anything other than a joy and a fulfilment comes in that little sentence which shows his weariness at finding himself among people for whom trusting in God comes hard, 'O *faithless* generation, how long shall I be with you, how long shall I bear you'.

We have looked at the evidence of the gospel stories, not the great dogmatic statements, but the assumptions behind the stories, the little asides, the unconscious claims that emerge in the texture and content of everyday conversations, and we are driven to see that the great dogmatic assertions really add nothing to them that is not there already.

The picture that emerges is, from one angle, that of a man, Jesus of Nazareth, a striking man, no doubt, yet one about whose ordinary humanity those who lived with him, slept at his side, ate and talked daily with him never for a moment entertained a shadow of doubt. Seen from another angle, however, here is someone who totally redirected his contemporaries' concept and experience of God, so that they could never again think of God apart from him, and so that those who had in the past shed their blood for the belief that there is but *one* who deserves the name of God ended up by bowing the knee to Jesus and giving him the honour due to God alone. And to return to the place where we began, this Jesus is not just a figure of the past, he is not just a universal figure spoken of with respect wherever he is named, but he is known alive today to millions of every nation and climate and tongue, and has imparted to those who worship God through him a personal focus and warmth of love that is found in no other form of religious devotion.

What are we to make of this extraordinary evidence?

The simplest thing is to try to avoid looking at it altogether and say it is all a fiction. Well, no respectable historian will back you there. But as soon as you begin to look seriously at the evidence, you are puzzled and fascinated and start trying to explain it.

It will not do, to begin with, to declare bravely that Jesus was simply an outstanding man and no more. He appears to have thought of himself as much more, and we cannot go on calling him good while taking no note of words and actions that in any other man would discredit all claim to goodness.

To call him a god-figure temporarily disguised in human dress, or a demi-god, half human, half divine, or a split personality — such 'explanations' have no meaning for us, and bear no relation to the compelling figure you meet in the Gospels.

In the end, after centuries of testing and rejecting one statement after another, the Church came up with a definition which does not, or course, make any attempt to 'explain' the mystery of Christ's person, but which does make clear within what limits any such attempt must lie. It said that, when we look at Jesus on the basis of the evidence available, we must maintain that he was indeed God in the same sense that God is God, while at the same time he was man in the same sense that we are men; that when we make these statements, we are talking about one and the same person all the time. Neither godhead nor manhood is in any way diminished or altered, nor are they dissolved together into some new amalgam, nor can they be taken apart so that some aspects of Jesus can be considered divine with others reckoned as just human. In everything this one person is fully both God and man. Christian faith is not tied to the language of that Chalcedonian definition, and every thinking generation will have another go, and will please some and upset others in the process. There will always be attempts to get simpler, more straight-forward explanations that will appeal to the commonsense man in the street, and our generation has seen some outstanding examples. But they usually achieve their results by failing to take seriously that this man was from birth completely at home with God in a way no other man has ever been and in a way that therefore requires some special explanation. Somehow, like the classic definitions, we have to say on the evidence of record and experience, that in Jesus Christ, God has spoken of himself in our human language with compelling love, with devastating challenge, and with a special and unique sort of finality.

Let me point to four brief implications of that assertion.

First, can we really take all this seriously?

We are in daily contact with hundreds of people for whom Jesus means nothing or next to nothing. Are they to be written off as of no account? We are aware of a great multitude of decisions, personal, local, national, international, being made all the time without any reference to things Jesus said or to any guidance he might be thought to be able to give. Can we really maintain a special significance for him? We take reverent note of the vast treasury of religious perception and experience in other faiths that give no place to Jesus but obviously have brought light to mankind in ways for which any unbiased observer can do nothing but thank God. Are they to be brushed aside? It may rightly be urged that where these other faiths bring divinity down to our human life, the figures involved, such as the Lord Krishna of Hinduism, cannot be argued to have shared our very human life as Jesus did, and where such religious leaders have been undoubted human figures, like Mohammed, they have never made claims to divinity remotely resembling those made by Jesus. But the question remains, how is it possible to maintain a uniqueness for Jesus without apparently devaluing all this great religious heritage? And we are further deeply and horribly aware of divisions among Christians themselves even in regard to the estimate to be given to Jesus, and does that not perhaps mean that we shall do better to keep quiet about the whole thing?

Yes, look from a *human* point of view at all the factors and circumstances of our *human* history and our contemporary *human* concerns, and it might well seem ludicrously inappropriate to try to make some plea for the special importance of that strange, perhaps not very significant figure of nineteen hundred odd years ago.

But let yourself once be tempted to give your attention seriously to him and reckon with the extraordinary things he seems to have said and done and claimed and demanded, and you may be led to wonder if perhaps here is not the very centre and key to all man's story, if there is not here God's very hand stretched out to point you to a way of making some sense of it all, and offering you a chance of coming at last to your home-base, and of going with the grain of the universe. Look seriously at Jesus and it will not be easy to write him off.

Secondly, there is an awkward thing about Jesus. Once you start paying attention to him, you begin to get hooked. You find it isn't just a matter of studying a very gripping figure of the past — it certainly is that, and the business gets more and more fascinating as you go along. But you soon become aware that Jesus puts pressure on you. He is not asking you to be interested in him, he is suggesting you must belong to him. You say, 'Don't be silly; I'm not that kind of a person, I'm not a church person, I'm not even a religious person', and you begin to have a horrid feeling that he isn't bothered if you didn't even go to Oxford or Cambridge, and he may not even have noticed the colour of your skin (and of course, his wasn't white either). Background or qualifications don't seem to matter. Jesus seems to be the sort of person who, once you begin to look at him seriously, demands that you make a response, and a total one and put yourself quite at his disposal.

Thirdly, if I am right to see Jesus as God speaking himself to us in our own language, then Jesus provides for us the essential definition both of God and of man. I think it is unarguable that all over the west, it is in fact Jesus who has determined the way we do tend to think of God, and even in the east, where there is a quite different starting-point, the compellingness of Jesus has again and again infiltrated Hindu and Buddist ideas. Similarly, in regard to the role, the rights and the responsibilities of men and women, it is Jesus who has set the essential pattern that we turn away from only to lose ourselves. To put it in a nutshell, all Christian theology flows from Jesus and has to be referred to him for its validation. Whenever the Christian church is in need of reform, whenever human life is in need of rejuvenation, whenever we are faced with new moral problems or unfamiliar human situations, we find ourselves looking for a focus again in Jesus. I have begun these lectures on the Christian faith with Jesus because this is where you must begin, and in every one of them I shall find myself referring back to him as the fount and touchstone of truth and right judgement. Jesus is every Christian's working definition of where you start from in every field.

And finally, this all means that what we know objectively of God, we know from the life he lived as a human being in the midst of our human life. Jesus turned up as God in a people specially chosen but by now pretty well down on its uppers, in a country not free but living under the heel of an occupying power, in a situation where his forerunner had been imprisoned for public criticism of the king, choosing men who had sick mothers-in-law, who were members of political activist groups or who were compromised by their involvement with their foreign masters. That is, God showed himself, not divorced from but utterly entangled in the actual web of historical human activity. And this means that anyone who decides he is going to go along with Jesus will not be finding an escape route from the problems of life in twentieth century Hull, rather he will be more closely involved with it all — as his spiritual life. There may indeed be times when you have to turn your back on the world in order to look only at God and so learn to see things straight again; it is certainly true that Jesus told men to be ready to lose the whole world for the sake of their real life with God. But his demonstration of God was worked out here, and he wouldn't have been crucified and so shown us God's real heart if it hadn't been. So if you think of turning to Jesus as an escape from the problems of the world today, think again. With Jesus, you will indeed see new visions, find new power, find you can begin again when you have failed, but with Jesus you will find also that you have to be more concerned than ever before with what goes into the Hull Mail every evening, international justice, with how you relate to your boss and to your equals, how you are behaving towards your wife and your children — and all these things will be your spiritual life. Jesus *is* the way in, but that way starts here and is worked out here, as he himself worked it out here.

So that's where we begin in this course — Jesus Christ, God saying to us all, 'Your human life, my human life, This is where I want to meet you. This is where I invite you to meet me' — and so to find for yourself firm ground under your feet, a direction for your lives and a hand stretched out — God's human hand.

God's World, or Whose?

Christian faith, I argued last week, required — among other things — a spiritual life worked out in this world.

But what is 'this world'?

Is it on your side, co-operating with your hopes? Is it against you, enemy and frustrater of all your good intentions? Or is it just there, neutral and uninterested background to whatever you think you may be doing? And indeed, does it really matter what you think about it at all? Well, first, two preliminary clarifications.

When we use the term 'the world' are we talking about the world of nature, 'The World About Us', or are we talking about that fascinating, swirling, organised, disorganised network of men and all their concerns, which provides 'News of the World'? or is it a mistake to distinguish the two?

In 1864, there was an outbreak of cattle plague in Wiltshire. The Vicar of Warminster, away on holiday in the South of France, wrote back to his congregation, 'I am very glad to hear that the services of repentance in the Minster are being well attended'. Clearly he thought that men and the created order were very intimately related, so that the prayers of men would affect the course of nature. And although we are today painfully trying to re-formulate that relationship in a way that takes account of the, at any rate, partial independence of science, it is evident that we are ourselves a part of the world of nature and cannot set out on any human project that does not involve the use of the materials of the world around us. So although it is possible to distinguish the world of nature and the world of men, and although sometimes one is emphasising one more than the other, I hope I shall be understood if I treat them both as essentially one world.

And obviously, the way you hear what I have to say will depend on how you feel the world has treated you and what you believe about it. But it is vitally important to ask whether we are world-affirmers or world-deniers, because this is not just an academic question.

It makes all the difference 'in the world' to the vigour and the hopefulness with which you pursue a course of action, whether you believe there is some overarching purposeful Providence working on the side of good, or whether you have resigned yourself to accepting that whatever you do, you are only floundering about in the mud of an indifferent universe that has no heart, no direction, no guiding principle to it. Our present pre-occupation with economics, in which we are not hearing the voice of any you could call prophets, means that we are constantly settling for short-term, pragmatic, trial and error prescriptions that offer no vision, stir no-one's blood, call forth no sacrifices. Contrast this, surprisingly enough, with the tone of the Brandt Report, dealing with international economic justice and development. Although the Commissioners came from different countries and no doubt had different beliefs, the whole Report seems to echo an unspoken faith in one integral world, where if you get the moral priorities right, the other problems can be solved — and so it has spurred hundreds of people to write to urge the British Government to take it more seriously, because it is a hopeful document. Clearly, it is important to ask 'God's World or Whose?'.

And then secondly, what sort of tone will you hear in my voice as I speak of 'the world'.

In the writings of the same St. John, we have the two conflicting verses, 'God so loved the world', and, 'Love not the world neither the things of the world'.

As a child, I had to recite a poem which began 'Great, wide, beautiful, wonderful world'. I don't think it was much of a poem, but it certainly set you off in a cheery mood. When I was older, I came across a Greek inscription which read, 'Hear lies So-and-So, son of So-and-So, would that my father and mother had never met', which testifies to the experience some have of the world as, bitter, unrelieved, hopeless, meaningless tragedy.

Three preliminary sketches.

In his Bampton lectures of 1978, called 'Creation and the world of science', Dr. A. R. Peacocke, a physical biochemist and a theologian, paints a fascinating picture of the emergence of our universe stage by stage, each stage arising out of its predecessor yet with no stage reducible to the terms of the last, and as the climax of the process, mankind, a society of intelligent persons able to reflect on the significance of the whole business. This appears to imply that the formation of man was implicit in the process from its chemical beginnings, and yet the process itself, because of the interplay of the fundamental physical constants and random features, is so delicate that at any stage a different reaction, say between protons, could have produced a totally different universe. This also means that the development of human persons appears to have been the aim of the process, and yet, when man begins to exercise his powers and reflect upon it, he is at once aware that he is not the cause of it. So Peacocke finds it proper to speak of a creator, of God, who is both immanent in the process, the energy that impels each element in it to realise the possibilities before it, but is also transcendent over it, in that it is his meaning and his intention that takes the process forward, his meaning which he wants to communicate to man, this crown of his creation who is able to share his thoughts and his hopes.

The second picture comes from the more recent science of ecology. It is now an accepted fact that the survival, certainly the health and fruitfulness of all living organisms depends on their achieving and maintaining the right dynamic balance with all the elements of the environment in which they are set. Cut down a forest of oak trees and replace it with another species, and it will shelter quite a different undergrowth cover of shrub and plant, which in turn will host a different society of small animals and birds, with the consequences that will have eventually for the fertility and the use of the surrounding land. Carry on up the scale, and it is clear that one major alteration in the general balance of nature in a particular area, and you can before too long produce quite a different economy. Before man began to flex his inventive and technical muscles in a big way, the natural world seems with reasonable security to have been able to digest minor ecological adjustments without serious consequences. But with increasing technical capacity, man now realises he commands increasing powers of devastation and is constantly upsetting balances and producing disasters he had no means of foreseeing. A brilliantly written conspexus of the whole interrelatedness of man and his environment is to be found, for example, in Barbara Ward and Rene Dubos' 'Only One Earth'. The sobering thing that has become increasingly apparent is that there is a morality in the scientific exploration and technical use of the earth's resources, a morality not defined simply by my need for survival, by the need of all my contemporaries for survival or even of all my successors for survival. It looks as if the earth itself makes a demand upon my reverence and understanding, I who have so much power over it — and where do I look for the definition of that?

A third picture might be the business men's picture of the world. Small businesses in an essentially agricultural, market town economy are easy to understand in largely personal terms, with, for example, the medieval church's laws against usury not too difficult to grasp, and sometimes, no doubt, even implemented. Then travel, communications and commerce expand, banking, ideas of administration and organisation develop, the industrial revolution bursts on the scene, and in a vast, new, industrial and commercial explosion, the one clearly identifiable principle is the profit motive, which at its best can no doubt be defended as the incentive for both the best quality product for the consumer, and the happiest industrial relations among all those involved in production. But the more the size of business grows, bursting across face-to-face local, then across national frontiers, the more personal leadership becomes remote from the production-force, the more pride in workmanship goes down before all the ingenuity of automation, the more industry is locked in the political struggles with pressures from governments on the one hand and from world economic forces on the other, and the harder it becomes to know whether to fight for profitability or for a more human dimension in labour relations, or to look for some other way of reconciling aims within industry itself, the more the whole enterprise realises that it is faced with the two alternatives of being simply a jungle at the mercy of predators each fighting for survival, or of discovering goals, structures and standards that will put a human heart into it all. And for this, self-interest, even enlightened self-interest, will not take you far enough, particularly if you think in the context of the rich and poor nations who make up our world.

These are only the briefest sketches out of many more needed to get a true picture, but they all emphasise three things — that the world of man and nature must be seen as an indissoluble whole, that in it man has a position of commanding but perilous eminence, and that standing on his dizzy height, he looks, or at any rate in his best moments he looks — for a principle of interpretation, a morality of meaning, a guiding Providence.

Last week I claimed that it is Jesus Christ standing in our midst who has defined for us the character and activity and purpose of God. Does he offer us anything like the principle we are looking for in *this* area? In an extraordinary moment of illumination, St. Paul says, if I may paraphrase him:

'Christ is the visible expression of the intention of God. He is the Elder Brother of everything created. He is the matrix from which everything took form, the End to which all tends, the principle by which all holds together.'

Marvellous but well-nigh incredible words to use of someone who was, after all, a young man.

But had Paul any justification for his words? Do they square with the gospel picture of Jesus? And if so, what does Jesus declare to us about God and man in relation to the world?

Jesus himself did not, of course, give a set of lectures on systematic theology in the City Hall, Nazareth, so we shall have to do with passing remarks, brief glimpses, recurrent emphases, but they do make up a consistent picture; and it will be sensible to distinguish between how Jesus paints God, and the way he expresses the responsibilities of being a man.

So his picture of God.

We can take it for granted that as a Jew brought up on the Old Testament tradition, Jesus accepted without argument that God was the Creator of the world: I say this because not all religions do accept this, and not all those who say they do really look as if they do.

But it is not just that Jesus accepted this — what interests us is to see what content he put into his belief.

I notice the following things.

In a prayer about a human situation which begins, 'I thank thee, Father, Lord of Heaven and Earth', you observe that God's care for man, heaven and earth is seen as one, and I think I should be right in seeing the term Father as inclusive of Lord of Heaven and Earth, to suggest a personal care for the whole.

Jesus himself is the vividest illustration of the Genesis declaration that what God created he saw to be good. It is material, created flesh he gladly and proudly wears to set forth God's whole glory. And at Christmas time we rightly dwell on the complete confidence in our humanity which God displayed in committing his Son to a woman's womb, and in entrusting his upbringing to this village girl and her relatives and to the homely wisdom of local schoolmasters and friends.

Jesus' parables show an observant and appreciative delight in all the ordinary doings of men and women going about their secular business and a familiarity with the seasons and processes of nature that form their natural background.

I argued last week that Jesus' miracles stem from a remarkable confidence that he walks in his Father's world, where evil and misery have no true place, and where, if he stands in his Father's will, he can defeat evil and allow nature to work for mankind's general benefit. He does not, for example, invite people patiently to put up with their sickness, but heals to show that it is health which is normal to God; and the so-called nature-miracles, the feeding of the multitude and the stilling of the storm suggest that at his hands nature does not impede but forwards the will of God.

And in the contemporary apocalyptic language Jesus is not ashamed to use to envisage his final coming as the gathering up of all things, he both identifies himself as the goal of the process and sees nature and historical circumstance as entwined together in the run-up; and we see him vindicated in advance in the physical resurrection on the third day.

Here then is the first thing that Jesus makes crystal clear. For him, God is the glad creator of all things and has no rival who is any more than a usurper where he does not belong; God honours and delights in his creation sufficiently to be ready to wear man's flesh for his greatest work, he is directing it all to fulfilment in Christ, and the attitude God shows to his whole creation can only be summed up in the word Father.

Now it is a very wonderful thing to maintain that this immense universe of universes, much of it still undiscovered by men, this whole complex of laws, interrelating forces and processes has a personal heart, and that this personal centre can be called Father, with the implication that he can be prayed to, that his will can be found and lined up with, that he himself watches over and presumably in some way directs the development not only of men but of the universe itself of which they are a part, and guides it to an ultimate fulfilment. Peacocke felt himself led towards this conclusion, but of course, Peacocke did approach his studies as a Christian already; others have wanted to believe it or have hoped it might be true, but did not know if they could trust their instincts; undoubtedly there are times when the immensity of the universe makes it hard to view it in personal terms and of course we make the task harder by limiting our use of the word 'personal' to our finite human experience of persons.

But we affirm that God is the creator and Lord of all things whom we properly call Father, because that is the way Jesus addressed him and thought of him, and the world responded to him as to one who knows he is at home in his Father's house.

And so we are brought to Jesus' portrayal of *man's* place in this world. And as his key word for God was Father, so his key word for man is Son. The Genesis story speaks of man as made in the image of God and as exercising dominion over the created world. Son both shows that image means family likeness and also describes the quality of that dominion. The son and heir to one of those fine old family estates both rejoiced in and was careful with its resources, learned stewardship from his father and exercised his father's authority, but as one of many concerned with the estate's management; he regarded the beasts and the pasture-land and the forestry, not just as materials for his own enrichment, but as part of his heritage, with the feel of it all in his bones, and with the obligation to understand its laws, to respect its particular demands and, indeed, to love it.

In the same way, I notice Jesus, by comparison with the ascetic John the Baptist, called a gluttonous man and a wine-bibber because he enjoyed the good things of life and the society of men and women with unaffected gratitude and pleasure, even though he was content to give them up when the will of his Father took him on the road of renunciation. Nature to him clearly has intrinsic worth, and I find it hard to think of him, even in an aside, dropping Paul's unlucky remark, 'Does God care for the ox?'. Rather, he says, 'Not a sparrow falls to the ground without your Father', and although the sentimental Franny Glass in Salinger's novel, *Franny and Zooey* cannot bring herself to say the next words, 'Are you not of more value than they?', Jesus has no doubt that there is a hierarchy of responsibility with man exercising the key role. He performs miracles, not as God, but as true man who understands God's mind and love for his creation, and so expects that, with evil dug out and banished, material nature is designed to respond positively to the good will of its creator. I doubt if to follow him requires us to think only in terms of miracle, or rather if we should not see the whole range of scientific, medical, technical and design activity, when exercised for the good of the rest of creation, as part of the way man animates the whole creation to respond in one great chorus of praise to God.

St. Paul — to redeem his good name — puts all this prophetically when he says that the whole creation groans and travails in pain until now, waiting for men to become *sons*, so that it too may be delivered from bondage to corruption and decay and find its own essential liberty. Jesus' picture of the world, answering to our three earlier sketches, shows God standing in the relation of Father to the whole universe, which therefore requires to be treated with its own appropriate reverence.

But man stands in the middle as son, responsible to God for it all, and for himself linked inextricably with it. There is no quick translation of these personal, pictorial images into the language of science and technology, no easy reading off from the New Testament of moral solutions to the complex issues of our world, but the pattern is this, and in labouring to apply it we have a recipe for a good world.

But, we can only leave the matter there by omitting one major consideration which alters the whole picture. Running right through the whole process is a fatal flaw, a poisoned seam, a streak of evil that puts a question-mark over everything we have so far said. If Jesus is right that it is God's world, with man marked to be his sons in it, how is it that the world meets us so often as incomprehensible, cruel and purposeless, and why is it, moreover, that Jesus, who so perfectly fulfilled man's role before God in his world, who overthrew evil and healed sickness, himself ended his days on earth the victim of a bitter, unjust and cruel death?

If we are to go on talking about God's world, we have to attempt to give some account of the terrible power of evil in it. Evil meets us in roughly four categories, and though we can point to some balancing goods, any one of them seems to make it a laughable folly to speak of God's world.

First, there is evil in nature itself and its processes. We have been arguing that the natural order is the creation of and reflects the nature of a good, wise, almighty Father. Earthquakes, floods, droughts, landslides, blight, suggest that the system is badly serviced or uncommonly accident-prone; while constant conflict between species that prey on one another for survival, and animal deformities and pain do not at once remind us of a father's care; and in spite of so much beauty and ingenuity, there is also in the process of nature a grimness, a cruelty, a heartlessness that one is hard put to give any account of. It may be argued, and rightly enough, that the flaws in nature have been the spur for the development of men's powers of inventiveness, imagination, bravery and compassion — just as it is equally true that man's carelessness and selfishness can intensify the effects of natural evil; it can be argued that it is the very question-marks in nature that have been the incentive to *scientists* to answer the questions and overcome the problems, and to *humanitarians* to provide for the victims of the cruelty. But should these benefits be purchased at such cost? Is disaster the only soil out of which such virtues can grow? Does the incidental good go anywhere near justifying the frightening underlying evil.

Then secondly, one must refer briefly to spiritual evil, a subject much more difficult to talk about.

It is only the over-dogmatic and the naive who are quite sure who or what they are talking about when they speak of the devil, but there certainly is a recognizable area of evil for which 'the devil' is a convenient shorthand, if no more. It is to be noted that scripture, as far as I can see, does not regularly make the devil the source of all evil, and indeed St. Paul can write the Epistle to the Romans, his greatest treatise on sin and salvation, without once mentioning the devil. And certainly the Bible nowhere thinks of the devil as God's opposite number, but rather sees God as the only author, creator, responsible initiator of *everything* — which, of course, partly makes the problem harder. But when you speak of the devil, you are asserting that you can sometimes be powerfully aware in actual experience that evil is not simply the absence of good, but is a perverse malignancy deliberately trying to corrupt or defeat you, that it sometimes appears to be the work of an organising intelligence, and that it can produce in you sensible fear and horror as at the presence of wickedness that cannot be opposed by merely human power. It is wise not to speak beyond one's actual experience here, and one should not invoke the devil, as is sometimes done, to excuse personal irresponsibility. But the experiences I have referred to are well enough documented, the malignant presence of spiritual evil is deeply frightening and is very hard to account for in a world that is the work of a good God.

Thirdly, what are we to make of the universal incidence of suffering and pain? Not all pain, of course, is intrinsically evil. If you train for the rugby season by running round Willerby in the early morning after your summer holiday, you can expect several days of excruciating aches and stiffness, but that won't of itself make you give up belief in a good God. I was with T. H. Somervell on the day of the report that Tensing and Hilary had at last conquered Mount Everest. Somervell had got to within one thousand feet of the summit without oxygen, and only turned back because he found the skin on the inside of his throat was beginning to flake off. He was a bit scornful of the two successful climbers for having achieved their ambition with the use of oxygen, having taken for granted that this kind of achievement can only be won by stretching the *human frame* to the limits of its endurance — though, of course, even he did not think Hilary and Tensing had had an easy ride. We accept that we have been given a raw-material universe in which to grow to our real potential, and that both growing and mastering the material involve painful and testing challenges to our human endurance — and on the whole we are ready to accept that this is a good thing. But who can see any good at all in the pain of children, the pain of the handicapped and immature; the suffering that seems to fall indifferently on those who deserve it and those who do not; the dreadful tortures men have inflicted on one another, the long, dragging, interminable pains that rob their victims of all human dignity; the pains continually suffered by the hungry and the oppressed; the needless, useless suffering caused to the innocent by the ignorance, stupidity and selfishness of their fellow-men?

Some have been ennobled by suffering, and their stories form some of the noblest pages of human history, but probably many more have been crippled and degraded by it, and there is altogether too much utterly unjustified and unexplained suffering and pain for any sensitive person to be able to accept *easily* that our life is watched over by a beneficent Father.

And fourthly, there is what one must simply call human sin, the whole heart-breaking catalogue of men's misdeeds that I have no intention of trying to list in detail. But there are some features of human sin that attention must be called to.

Why is it, for example, that right from the start it seems easier to do wrong than right? One might think it was simpler to tell the truth than to lie until one has met the surprising deviousness of little children and primitive people. Why is it that the earliest processes of childhood seem to engender self concern, fear, jealousy and the spiteful willingness to hurt those who want to play with my toys? Why is it that we can hardly conceive of pure feelings of desire, but that the stirring of the imagination of the flesh seems so quickly burdened with guilt? Why is it that we do not, as our first instinctive speech, *pray* to God, but have to be *taught* to do what we are then told is our true nature? No doubt, a great deal of the blame can be laid at the door of our environment, so that a child is born into an atmosphere with a down-drag already in it, but that is surely only to push the problem back further. Why is it that we claim that we are God's creatures, but apparently from the start are found looking in the opposite direction, with a predisposition to *respond* to the temptation rather than to resist it, or better still not to notice it there?

Then, how can we estimate the significance of ignorance in human unhappiness? Our generation accuses our grandfathers of exploitation in some field or another because they were simply unaware of some factor now seen to be significant. They thought they were showing commendable inventiveness. If it is true that again and again we simply did not know that this action would be followed by these consequences, why do we feel guilty about it? You may remember the old naval saying, 'It's no excuse to say I didn't hear the pipe'. Why does one part of us tell us that this is unfair, and another part tell us it is true?

Again, we could very well describe the whole glory of man in terms of his perversions — qualities of leadership turned into tyranny, strength of purpose into obstinacy, intelligence into arrogance, appreciation of the riches around us into greed and lust, faith in God turned into self-confident dogmatism, love turning into jealously or dissolving into apathy and boredom. And in every perversion of his greatness, man involves others and the materials of the world in his misdeeds, lays himself open to further corruption, and so tightens the whole network of evil around him and binds it more firmly on the world.

But perhaps the greatest heartbreak of all is that from time to time a man catches a glimpse of what he might be, and all his heart tells him that is what he ought to be and was created to be; and yet he knows, or by bitter experience comes to discover, that there is simply no chance whatever of his coming within shouting distance of these visions of truth. A fine young hero dedicates his life to the overcoming of some injustice. By the purity and single-mindedness of his devotion he wins others to work with him. They make sacrifices and are bound together into a warm fellowship of trust as they stand side by side to meet the early opposition and are able to join together and defeat it successfully. But as they press on, the leader discovers there is unpleasant rivalry among his friends, he learns that one is plotting to betray the movement for personal advantage, another can't stand the pace and is losing interest, and his own leadership is increasingly coming under criticism — and when he examines his own heart, he realises it is no longer pure, other idols have crept in, and the original goal, if indeed he ever really saw it, has been lost sight of or has faded — despaired of or abandoned. He began believing in the possibility of perfection, is corrupted on the way from without and within and ends with a tarnished mediocrity and no undimmed flame in his heart to set against it. Is there any great movement whose history I have not described in those few sentences? Man made in the image of God. It this all it amounts to? God's world or whose?

It is a proper question.

The question in fact resolves itself into three:

First, where does evil come from in a world said to be created by God?

Secondly, can anything be said in mitigation of the picture I have painted above? Can we claim this world is the best of all possible worlds in spite of the flaws in it?

And thirdly, where does all this leave us?

First then, where does evil come from? Four answers have been advanced:

Evil, some have maintained, is essentially an illusion. Put on the true spiritual spectacles and it will disappear. This answer takes seriously our instinctive feeling that evil is less true, less normal than good, and some religions have been made up on the basis of this premise, but no person in serious trouble ever found it rang true. The old limerick put its finger on its weak point long ago:

> There was a faith healer of Deal
> Who said, Though I know pain's not real
> When I sit on a pin
> And puncture my skin,
> I dislike what I fancy I feel.

Evil is no illusion. It is a terrible and immediate reality, which cannot be dissolved with wishful thinking.

Others have maintained, and all of us at times seem almost driven to maintain, that we live in a dualistic world, with God and evil locked in constant and maybe equal conflict, with no certainty of the outcome. Manichaeism and Zoroastrianism took this as their basic tenet, and even Christians have sometimes tended to elevate the devil to a position he never has in scripture and make him a co-equal power with God. But the great religions of the world have never taken this position, and the Bible is quite paradoxically clear on the point: 'I form the light and I make the darkness, I make peace and I create evil, I the Lord do all these things'. The Bible allows ultimate responsibility to none but God, the one alone with any power to create. Evil may be a terrible power, but it is less real than God, and does not share his eternity. It does not exist from the beginning with him, and it is somehow subordinate to him.

Others have held that evil is a leftover from our evolutionary history, a testimony to our animal origins. But this is a particularly weak theory. We have no clear evidence among animals of the consciousness of right and wrong; when we accuse a man of being beastly, we are usually quite gratuitously attributing to him a nastiness we do not see among animals but only among men; and the really monstrous evils among us are those that arise not in our animal nature, but in that part of us we do not appear to share with the animals, our minds, our imaginations, our spirits. Evil is not a leftover from our animal past, rather the more man advances, the greater seems his capacity for evil.

The most developed Christian attempt to explain the origin of evil is the doctrine of the Fall, which emerged from St. Augustine's treatment of the story of the serpent tempting Adam and Eve to eat the apple in the Garden of Eden. This is a very profound doctrine, in that it does try to give an account of the fact that we all appear to be born with an inherited fascination for sin, an inherited weak will in regard to it, and an inherited guilty conscience. The doctrine of the Fall does insist what all our instincts tell us, that my sin is part of the network in which I am found together with all those around me and all those who went before me, and that I am not a free, independent agent, even though I carry my own personal burden of guilt for my part in it all. The doctrine goes further, and in the sentence, 'Cursed be the ground for thy sake', maintains that man in his fall pulled nature down with him, thus arguing that fallen man and the flawed creation form one tangled web of corruption. These are profound if disturbing insights, but as an explanation of the origin of evil, the doctrine of the Fall fails at two points. First, while there is plenty of evidence that men and men, and men and nature, are locked together in one network of misfortune and evil, there is no scientific or historical evidence of a paradisal state from which they fell. The earliest man we know of made weapons to fight his neighbour with, and the oldest fossils bear witness to strife between the species: creation seems to have been fallen from the start. Moreover, Genesis gives no account of how the serpent, the tempter got into the story in the first place. Descriptions of the devil as an angel who fell through pride leave unanswered the question of why such a temptation should ever be found in heaven and where it came from.

No we are left with the uncomfortable conclusion that in a world we want to claim on the authority of Jesus as made good by God, the origin of evil that smears and mars it all is unexplained. There never has been and it seems probably there never will be any satisfactory account of the origin of evil.

Question number one remains disturbingly unanswered.

Our second question was, 'Are there any arguments that can be urged to justify the presence of evil in the world'?

Well, it is possible to argue that evil is only the inevitable negative aspect of three positive goods we should never want to surrender.

First, it has been argued that evil, and particularly man's own wrong doing is the inevitable counterpart of his freedom. There is no virtue if one is compelled to exercise it, no goodness if it is performed by robots, no love except what is freely given and can be just as freely withheld. To be a man is to be free, so that the slave is wounded in his essential nature. We take precautions to protect our children but in the end we let them come to harm rather than rob them of their inherent freedom. We define human rights in terms of freedom, and we thereby unconsciously assume that freedom allows a man not to do what others want of him or even what is best for himself. We take it for granted that if the only goodness there is is goodness freely chosen then there must be an alternative evil to choose from. In all this we are saying that if evil is the price of our freedom, then we would rather accept a world with evil in it than surrender that precious freedom. When we look at the extent and horror of evil, it seems a high price to pay, and in any case is the basic premise of the argument sound? It is true that in the world *as we know it*, we can only exercise our freedom by choosing between good and evil, but that is the point: is ours the only conceivable world; could there not have been a better one; God himself is presumably freer than any human being, but he does not seem to need the choice between good and evil in order to maintain his freedom. C. S. Lewis in *Perelandra* tried to picture a world in which people were tempted but did not fall, remained free without sin.

Secondly, one thing the whole network of evil makes blindingly clear is that God, man and the world are meant to be a unity. The terrible tangle of evil that jangles all the gears of the universe, breaks its natural harmonies and produces grinding discords demonstrates better than anything else that the whole created order was made to be one brotherhood of love, singing one song of praise, gathered in one great eucharist of worship. Evil arises through the failure of all to realise the one law of love, and it is indeed evil itself that cries out most loudly for a world healed and at one. If this is true, however, it hardly makes the problem of evil easier. For it seems to imply that there is no ultimate hope for any one component part, for any one individual, unless there is one plan of redemption for all.

And thirdly, we have already argued that long before we face the actual problem of evil, we recognise that we have been set in a world designed to challenge and stretch us, a world where prizes are won through risks taken, a world where progress is made because plainly it is raw materials and not the finished products we are given to work with, a world where certain advances can only be made through sweat, tension, toil and pain. And even when the factor of evil mysteriously creeps into the natural cragginess of the world given to us, we are driven to admit that it is the very flaws and horrors in man's world that have evoked his noblest responses — his most brilliant inventions to overcome them, his qualities of bravery and endurance to bear them, all his tenderness and compassion to care for their victims, and his glimpsing of the ultimate virtue of self-sacrifice as a way of healing their hurts. The world is a better place for all those unmarried daughters who have given up hope of personal fulfilment in order to remain at the side of a sick, aged or complaining parent. Yes, the pain of the world is more than matched by the human greatness it has called forth, and it is the response to evil more than any other single factor we can point to that has raised man to the heights of his nature. But, but, but . . .

It may indeed be said that the potential glory of man and the world, the whole divinity of the enterprise is seen only more brilliantly against the dark background of evil; it may indeed be said that we would not wish to live in a world where men needed no such stimulus to greatness. But is this really convincing? Can any amount of human heroism be set in the balance as a justification for one deformed child? Are we not bound to ask if this is indeed the best of all possible worlds, if God could not have produced the same results by less devastatingly cruel means?

We began by arguing that this is God's world, with Jesus himself as our strongest argument.

But we have not found a way of explaining how evil got into the system; and it is not easy to be persuaded that the arguments advanced to justify its presence are really as satisfactory as we should wish.

I have stated the problem of evil as strongly as I could, maybe overstated it, because Christians are sometimes tempted to rush to the defence of God by minimising its fearfulness, and by smart answers to hope the problem will go away.

To such people, Job of old in his pain said, 'O that you would altogether hold your peace, and it would be your wisdom; miserable comforters are ye all'.

But have I not destroyed my case that we live in God's good world? So our third question is, 'Where does all this leave us?'.

Shall we say, 'Bother the whole business: eat drink and be merry, for tomorrow we die'?

Shall we, with the stoics, say, 'There is no help from outside ourselves: let us bear bravely the yoke that has been fastened upon us, accept our fate in a heartless world, and for our own pride's sake with no hope of gain or any eternal reward show our fellows what man unaided can be'?

'In the fell clutch of circumstance
I have not winced nor cried aloud;
Under the bludgeonings of chance
My head is bloody, but unbowed.'

No, neither of these solutions corresponds to the deepest instincts in us.

We want an answer.

We don't just want words; we want an answer for the heart.

We want an answer from God.

He must tell us if it is, nevertheless, his world, and if so, what we are to make of it as it is.

We turn to him, sometimes shaking our fists in anger, sometimes wonderingly questioning, sometimes brokenly praying, sometimes mysteriously hoping, since he surely cannot disapprove of our asking and we say, 'You are responsible for all this. Is it nothing to you that we suffer, and that your world — if it is your world — mocks you for your inability to meet it at its greatest point of need? What do you expect us to make of it all?'.

And it seems to me, God, that great father of it all, accepts that he is responsible, he and no other, and that it is his business to get us to see the meaning of it all through his eyes, and to know that we are met and answered.

He first points to the instincts he has planted in us that good is more natural than evil, that it is more normal to be well than ill, that love is true and hatred is false, that justice is mighty and will prevail, and that these instincts are themselves a vote for him; he points to all the healing processes built into the fabric of the universe, to the very restorative effects of time itself, all of them evidence of his benevolent care; and he urges us not to overlook the beauty in reaching for the ugliness.

He reminds us of what he has actually shown us of himself, as we have already seen, in Jesus Christ, who neither tolerated nor accepted evil and pain, but drove out devils and healed the sick, and so showed health, happiness, freedom and goodness to have the backing of God.

But beyond, and deeper than all this, in his coming among us, he stepped unflinching into the arena of our misery, and from within the vortex of injustice, rejection, pain and death, set up a universal Instrument of Healing that has altered the complexion of the whole problem to any who have tasted its medicine.

An Instrument of Healing

Last week I was passionately arguing that the world we live in, with all the marvellous inter-connectedness of man and nature, is the creation of God who designed it in joy and delight for growth, for freedom and for harmony. Yet this claim seems to be mocked by the great streak of evil running through it at every level and turning its intended harmonies into jarring discords. Nevertheless, I argued that God accepts that he and no other has the ultimate responsibility for the world even as it is, and since man's own misdeeds and sin seem to form the key to the rest of the creation's corruption, it is at that point that God steps in with a strange instrument of healing and alters the complexion of the whole thing.

Now it is sometimes said that Christians spend too much time harping on the sinfulness of man, emphasising his weakness rather than his greatness, and that in doing so they fail to respect his inherent nobility, and treat him as a cripple needing always to be helped over stiles rather than as a hero whose occasional lapses simply need to be forgiven and forgotten. It is further said that this obsession with man's failings has led Christians into extraordinary and morally unbelievable theories of atonement for sin, of the need for blood-sacrifice as the only way of appeasing the righteous anger of a just God — whereas with our own children we require no such extreme measures, but simply forgive and restore them. Does not this fixation on sin, and-death-as-the-penalty-for-sin, deny everything we claimed last week, give a grim and gloomy picture of God and an essentially negative view of man, so that any claim that the Christian gospel is good news can only begin to sound credible to those who are at the end of their tether?

I think it must be admitted that the way in which Christians have *sometimes* talked about sin does imply a low view of man, painting him as a patient who without continually turning up in the surgery will inevitably relapse into sickness, rather than as one for whom to be normal is to be healthy. I remember pulling the leg of a splendid, but somewhat over-scrupulous doctor friend of mine and saying, 'It says in the

Bible that God saw that everything he had made was good: you don't believe that, you think it ought to be boiled first'. It is true that some ways of speaking about God's work of redemption have an unhealthy flavour about them — as if Christians were saying, 'As long as there is weakness and sin about, we're in business'. It is partly to exclude such views that I was at pains to insist that it is God's world, the world God is proud of, that we live in, and that the view of man that he gave us in his Son Jesus Christ is a breath-takingly high one.

It cannot be too strongly emphasised that the doctrine of redemption, while properly concentrating on the grim seriousness of man's sin, should not fail to be a constant reminder of the glory sin spoils, nor fail to engender confidence that the process of healing will in the end bring an even more wonderful fulfilment to God's design than it might have had without that fatal flaw. But to suppose that the evil and sin that infiltrates and stains and warps every level of man's activity can be dismissed as occasional lapses, or can be dealt with by the easy formula, forgive and forget, is to live blinkered in a fool's paradise, and simply not to be aware with any sensitivity of what happens around us all the time.

Let me take five examples of the effect that sin has — and that forgivness hardly gets anywhere near. And I will take them, not from horror films or out-of-the-ordinary experiences, but from situations all of us find ourselves in.

Think of a father and a son, the father strict in his views, loving his son, determined to bring him up well, surrounding him with too much advice, requiring an account from him for every minute out late; the son, admiring his father, knowing he is concerned for his good, suffocated by his care, deliberately kicking over the traces and aggravating things by rudeness in order to establish his independence. Bit by bit, they get to the stage where these two good men can't talk to one another, where the springs of love are choked by resentment, where every attempt at conversation begins with an implied criticism. How do you restore that relationship which sin, infecting good intentions, has ruined? The question of forgiveness hardly gets on to the agenda. Either might forgive the other if the other admitted he was in the wrong, but neither can accept that it is he who needs to be forgiven. And would a word of forgiveness obliterate all that backlog of indignation and resentment? Isn't some stronger medicine needed?

Again, think of the people who throng the psychiatrist's consulting room, or the counsellor's study or the confessional. Guilt. Some wrong act in the past has been allowed to fester: it has stained the memory, infected the subconscious, damaged the capacity for relationships, weakened the will, made it hard for the person to believe that he can ever escape from the net of it and not fall again. It may well be that it is forgiveness that is needed to dissolve the crippling effect of guilt, but if so, it will need to be a whole lot more than the cheery word, 'Don't worry about it, let's forgive and forget'. Forgiveness will have to go down deep, discover the canker, and heal the poisoned springs. And who has the power to forgive like that?

Thirdly, sin has consequences that no amount of forgiveness can recall. Do you remember the novel and film 'Term of Trial'? A school master gives extra lessons to a teenage girl, and does not notice that she is developing a strong passion for him. On the boat on the way back from a school outing to Paris, she comes into his cabin at night and offers herself to him. When, taken aback and shocked to the core he hustles her back to her own cabin, her sense of rejection turns her love to fury, and with her mother's connivance, she takes a case against him for indecent assault. In spite of everything that can be said, the evidence is so damning that it is clear he will be condemned, until finally the girl breaks down and admits in court that she made it all up. The teacher is cleared of all charges, but after the hooha has died down, the headmaster says to him, 'Well, I think for the sake of the school's good name, it would be best if you looked for a job elsewhere', and in the final scene, his wife says, 'Well now that it's all over, tell me what really happened'. The girl's one passionate lie has ruined an innocent man's career irretrievably: he is forgiven but destroyed.

Or again, think of the man who after making a bit of money by a variety of dubious means, decides at last that he has had enough of it all and wants to go straight and he now wants to go into public life. Well, there are an awful lot of people who know too much about his past, who were his partners in some of his more doubtful enterprises, to whom he still owes favours for past help, and who will certainly ask him to turn a blind eye to any shady business of theirs if he comes to any position of authority. As he looks back at the past, he realises that he can't get free from it to do any good in the future. He is bound to others by the ties of former misdeeds, and entangled with others who can hold him back from following the right path he wants to tread. Unless there is some clean sweep of all his former accomplices, he will live all the time weakened in his resolves by the fear of blackmail, by the chains of his own misdoings.

And finally, the most heartbreaking result of sin is that it has quite simply dragged down the level of expectation of the whole human race. No-one expects perfection, and we have reached the bitterly ironical situation where we budget for mediocrity and failure by saying, 'After all it's only human'. To err is human — what sort of creed is that in face of the glory set before us? Sin has brought us to accept lowered sights, to settle for second-rate solutions and cynically to mock the idealists, because we have no hope of ever reaching a perfection that in our hearts we know is the only real truth. Where does forgiveness come into the calculation at all?

Grim irretrievable consequences. And while we have these days tinkered about with our consciences more than is good for us, it comes home to us from time to time that it is God we have offended and are accountable to, and we rightly sense that, Father as he is, it is not in his nature to turn a blind eye to wickedness or to sweep sin under the carpet. We have heard it said that he hates the sin but loves the sinner, but in our clearer moments we recognise that sin has no existence except in sinners, and wonder what will be left of the sinner when finally God acts to turn out this sin in his world.

And standing and looking at the whole smudged picture, man trapped by his sins and at bay cries out, 'Can't we rub it all out and start again' — and knows you can't. He longs for a solution that will, as it were, tear the offending pages out of the book, and bring him back again to where he was with a clean sheet and a fresh start — and knows he longs in vain.

It is not so long ago that a distinguished M.P., tangled beyond recall in the irretrievable mess of his affairs, had his death announced and arranged for a pathetic private resurrection for himself in Australia under another name. He saw no escape from the toils of his situation and heard the words 'death settles all scores' as the only solution.

And at this point, the Christian doctrine of the atonement begins to sound a little less outlandish and irrelevant, for it is an attempt to meet that agonised and longing cry, an offer from God of a way of rubbing the whole slate clean and starting again. And in *this* context perhaps it is neither foolish nor morbid to talk about death, or something corresponding to death, and in particular the dying and rising of Christ.

But before turning to what Jesus actually did, let us briefly examine this dying and rising model with a couple of illustrations. Imagine a private school, that once had a good name, but which has now gone badly downhill: an old headmaster, a drop in teaching standards, bad relations in the staff-room, poor discipline and a series of incidents in which the headmaster finds a number of teachers more sympathetic to the offending pupils than loyal to him. How can the situation be remedied? With all the obvious difficulties, troublesome boys are punished and opportunities taken to move disloyal staff on. But the rot has gone too deep; stronger measures are met with unco-operative resentment, and new staff-members are soon infected with the old atmosphere. The headmaster's retirement gives the governors a chance to appoint a younger, stronger man, but when he fails to carry staff and students with him and finally resigns in face of a hopeless task, what options are left to the governors? They take the extreme course, announce that with due notice staff and students will be dispersed and the school will be closed, with the intention that after a suitable interval it will be reopened with an entirely new staff and intake. Death and resurrection.

But notice two features of this illustration. The first is that successive attempts to remedy matters by dealing with one pupil here and one staff member there might perhaps have worked in the early stages of trouble, but by the time the infection has got into the system as a whole, any attempt to tackle the evil must tackle it as a whole. No piece-meal solution will work — only an all-embracing one. And that leads to the other paradox. The closure may indeed have purged out the evil and brought new life to that abstract entity, the school. But as far as the staff and students who were involved in it are concerned, the remedy has no dimension of hope for them. They may have accepted that they deserved a share in the dismantling of the school, but the remedy provides no place for them in the school's rising from the ashes. The death had been a death for them. Any resurrection is for somebody else, not them.

Turn now from this imaginary school to the actual situation of God's Israel, under the kings — sinning themselves further and further away from God, flirting for political reasons with foreign gods, abandoning the old puritanical morality of the desert for the luxuries and immoralities of the settled life. One prophet after another arises to castigate them, urging that if only they will repent and turn back, God will withhold the judgement he otherwise must bring upon them. It fell to Jeremiah to declare, after twenty-three years of ministry battling away with the sinful people he loved, after seeing one flash-in-the-pan movement of repentance after another die away without making any essential difference to the direction of the national life, that the whole national conscience had become too blunted for any serious repentance to be any longer an imaginable possibility. In these circumstances, Jeremiah says that, like a potter taking the flawed clay off the wheel and squashing it back into a lump and starting all over again, God is going to uproot the people he has planted out of the holy land, drive them into the darkness of the pagan idolatory they have just lusted after, destroy the apparatus of their deadening religion, and let exile and the death of the nation work upon them as the only way of purging the evil out of them — and then when a whole generation has passed away, raise up a fresh generation of those who will seek the Lord with a new heart and bring them back home to a new beginning. Once again in extreme circumstances, we see that, while there were good men and godfearers in Israel before the exile, eventually only the death of the nation as a whole has any chance of overcoming the inbred corruption; *and once again*, while some resented the exile and only a few saw its meaning, and while evil and good alike had to bear its purging fires, neither the one nor the other survived for the resurrection; only an entirely new generation enjoyed that. Death indeed acted as a remedy; but there was no new birth for those whose sin required that remedy.

These two illustrations show that when sin has really got its grip on a situation, warnings, offers of forgiveness and individual attempts to do better are in the end insufficient, ineffective and marginal in their effects. Some sort of death is the only way in which the canker in the whole system can be attacked and overcome. Repentance and forgiveness do not deliver the individual penitent *from the situation*, do not strike at the root of his predicament. Only a total remedy affecting the situation as a whole can offer the individual any real hope of a new start. But in the models I have used, the tragedy is that for the sinner, even the penitent sinner, who is involved in the great act of purging by destruction, that is the end. Others may benefit later, but not he. He may be the very one who most clearly sees that only the rubbing out of the whole situation will allow for a new start, but because he is a part of that whole to be rubbed out, for him, this remedy brings no new start, only destruction.

We seem at a deadlock. Is there no way out?

And it is at this point that people have begun very tentatively to ask, would it be possible for some champion from outside to enter into the sinner's situation and undergo the purging death on his behalf in a way that enabled the sinner, after all, to begin again. It doesn't take long to see that, in human terms, this is not possible. For in the first place, it would require someone who is exactly in the sinner's position, up to his neck in sin, recognising that he deserves the wages of wrong doing, totally entangled in his condition, and yet able somehow to represent *all* those involved — for it would be morally offensive and essentially ineffective if some innocent outsider offered himself as a dramatic stand-in for the guilty and bore the extreme penalty that would be entirely extrinsic to him, nor can one imagine the sort of representative who could properly act and suffer on behalf of *all* the guilty; and in the second place, in what sense could such a substitute really be said to have dealt with the trouble at all? He might have delivered each sinner from the actual penalty but in fact it is that very death that the sinner himself knows to be his only healing; he wouldn't have altered the situation around the freed sinner, who would thus find himself exposed to the same temptations as before, and his brave act would be no more than a fragrant but thin example, with no power to help the sinner against future delinquency. There have been repeated attempts to find human parallels to show how an external redeemer might take the saving death upon himself, while allowing the sinner the chance of new life, but they remain unconvincing, morally unsatisfactory and practically irrelevant.

It is at the point where we have caught some glimpse of the one remedy whereby the stranglehold sin has over mankind might be broken, and yet have found ourselves driven into deadlock since the remedy destroys the very people it is designed to help, that we turn to look at the work Jesus Christ is said to have done among us. Now the death of Jesus can be understood from many different angles, but it is as God's remedy for sin that it is most profoundly spoken of.

Here there are five things to call attention to.

First, in the first lecture I argued that in Jesus *God* was expressing himself among us. That is to say, what Jesus does is both an expression of God's eternal nature and character, and also has the quality of a divine act, that is, it is universal in its scope and complete in its effectiveness. If, therefore, we can properly interpret Jesus' death and resurrection as intended to be an act of atonement, then it will be something done by God for all men, all-sufficient and universally valid.

Secondly, at the outset of his ministry, Jesus was baptised by John with 'a baptism of repentance for the remission of sins'. How could Jesus undergo such a baptism? — unless it might be claimed that he went to the Jordan bearing the sins of others. Is this idea of bearing the sins of others a credible concept of which we have any experience? Yes, most surely it is. If a good father learns that his well brought-up son has been arrested on charges of shop-lifting or drug-pushing, who is likely to feel the greater weight of guilt, father or son? — probably the father. And notice first, that the more upright the father is, the more ashamed and guilty he will feel; a corrupt father might say, 'Silly fellow to get caught';

and secondly, the more the father loves the boy the more *he* will feel that he is to blame for the boy's misdeeds: if father and son are out of touch with one another and the father only reads about the arrest in the paper, he will be upset, no doubt, but not so desperately ashamed. A just father cannot but bear the sin of the son he loves. John the Baptist summoned Israel to repent, and because of his oneness in heart with Israel and by his identification with his Father's righteous will, Jesus, more than anyone else, can feel the bitter shame of Israel's alienation from God, so with a deeper blush and a more aching heart he can come to God as Israel, in penitence, and confess the sin that Israel herself is hardly any longer conscious of.

In Jesus we have someone who is right at our heart, standing in with us, feeling the weight of our alienation, bearing our sin — but not yet, of course, bearing it away.

Now when we go into a dirty situation intending to try to pull it round, we normally like to limit the field, ally ourselves with a particular band of goodies and hold the baddies at arm's length while we get established. But Jesus takes them all to be Israel and settles in with them all — he preaches in synagogues and heals churchwardens' daughters, eats with Pharisees and argues with intelligent scribes, but he also touches and heals the repulsive, is at home with the finger-print classes, calls disciples off the streets and behaves as God's Israel with them all. He treats them all with that marvellous respect that supposes they will all want to respond to God. Well, they like it at first and warm to him, and suppose he will take up their causes. But after a bit they all come to realise that he is taking it too seriously, expects them to be God-first men all the time and in everything, expects God actually to work — even in church. So some simply melt away into the background, others see they had better make a determined attempt to get rid of him, and his closest disciples shudder at the distrust they see coming. And while in gentle words and harsh ones, in private conversation and public diatribe, in compassionate healings and in nationwide campaign, he never ceases to try to galvanise them into being Israel, equally he never abandons them when they abandon him, never accepts them as enemies when they decide he is their great enemy, never loses the sense of total identification with them when they become quite alienated from him. Just because he could never stand aside from them but remained their own best self, so he is more and more enmeshed in the tangles of their apathy, malice, hopelessness and plain wickedness. When he came to his trial, no one stood up for him, yet he stood there for them, the Messiah they ought in their hearts to have been waiting for and wanting. In an extraordinary phrase, St. Paul says, 'Him who knew no sin he made to be sin for us'. Read the gospels and you can see the process taking place.

Thirdly, not only did Jesus foresee that his mission would take him to his death, not only did the cross cast a shadow over the latter part of his ministry, but he did say something by way of interpreting the meaning he gave to that death. He saw it not as an accident or a tragedy, but as divine necessity. It is easy to misunderstand this. People sometimes say that Jesus came to earth in order to die so that the scriptures might be fulfilled, and paint his human life as of no interest to him in his race to get to the cross. I have already stressed how glad Jesus was to live a human life and — to describe the impossible — nothing would have given him greater pleasure than if men had responded to him and his death had been unnecessary, or if at any rate his *disciples* had sufficiently grasped the meaning of his passion to want to share it with him. But of course his death was a necessity just because the inbred corruption of men made these two options impossible and made us unable to bear the total holiness and goodness of God, or do other than determine to get rid of him. Scripture too, in the great passion psalms, foresaw that a spiritual movement is in the end betrayed by those who are most closely associated in it, but this does not mean that Jesus called Judas just to have someone to fulfil that role. Christ's death was a necessity, and a necessity foreseen, but there is nothing mechanical here: the events leading up to his death are of the kind that many a brave leader on a similar course has known he would have to face. Yet Jesus does not see this necessity just as a piece of grim inevitability to be borne; he sees it as something positive being done. In the course of a discussion with his disciples, he speaks of himself as a slave willing to go to the extent of laying down his life as a ransom — to buy men out of the clutches of their slavery. He sees his death as in some sense opening a gate of liberation for men. Then again, in his last meal with his disciples he describes the bread and the wine he gives them as the broken body and the shed blood of the covenant-sacrifice required to open a whole new chapter in the relations between God and men. Now no longer the Jews alone — by this sacrifice, all men are to become God's specials, a covenant that will bring in the stranger from the field, the lost from the wilderness, the outcast and the alien into the family, and will sit them all down at the table with God. Jesus did not see his death simply as something done to him, but rather as something done by him, the climax of all his coming meant, with a positive, victorious, liberating quality to it.

Fourthly, it is an amazing thing to watch Jesus actually going to his death. Let us recall that Jesus was not arrested for being a quiet nonentity, not just for speaking good words and for doing kind deeds. He was arrested because he would keep trying to get Israel to take being Israel with complete seriousness, when everyone else either thought he was going too far or wished he'd be quiet, or was an uncomfortable threat to those already in authority or was doing something politically suicidal. He was arrested for public activity in the name of God, by those who feared his popularity and wanted to brand him as an imposter. He was arrested because he took it for granted that God was the most important reality in life, and because he cared enough for men to want them to believe it with him. In his trial we see him pressed to the limit to maintain these attitudes of trust and love. He stood silent in the face of slanderous and provocative accusations, because to have leapt to his own defence might have led into the kind of bickering in which he sharpened his tongue and began to treat his opponents as enemies, and he will not do that. When he is finally condemned, on what were undoubtedly unproven charges, he neither curses, threatens nor lashes out at his judges. On the cruel cross, when one might have expected pain to concentrate all his faculties on himself, we see him praying for his tormentors, thinking of his heart-broken mother and responding marvellously to a flicker of faith in one of those crucified with him; and as the darkness of death, the despised failure's death, the solitary imposter's death settles upon him, he is praying to an apparently stony God above. He need never have been there at all; his only crime was that he loved men to a point they could not bear, trusting that he was acting in this for God. At the end, when there was no further activity open to him, he died in naked, comfortless trust, handing it all over to a God he could not feel, experiencing in himself nothing but the bitter hopeless god-forsakenness of the blind uncomforted sinner's death. Trust in God to the limit; identification with us to the uttermost, and because that uttermost was without reprieve, that trust and that love dragged Jesus Christ down into sinful mankind's deserved grave. In all of this, he was in it with us.

And the fifth thing, of course, is that, beyond the possibility of anyone's expectation, God vindicated him, saying 'This Jesus was what I am, what I mean and what I do', and brought him out of the grave. He raised him to a new inviolable, life all the efforts of sin and death lying defeated in ruins behind him, a new life available for us men whom he had taken to himself. Now it's hard to say in logical terms exactly what that death effected, what is the mathematics by which we can calculate its result, but the first simple fact is that the disciples who were closest to him and so had betrayed him worst and were most guilt-stricken, discovered when he found them after the resurrection, with a deeper shame than they had ever experienced before and a deeper joy and freedom than they had ever conceived possible, that that failed past was behind them, that in some way he had died their death, and that they were sharers of his new life, indeed they were the trusted apostles of his new life. They weren't perfect, they still made mistakes, they still quarrelled, because they hadn't in literal fact died his crucial death. But bit by bit they let his new life overtake their old life, and identification with him become the new reality arising from the ashes of the old.

Here, then, at the heart of human history was a death of the dimensions we have been groping after. It was died by a man who came from God, and so it has an absolute quality about it; it was died by one who bore no guilt of his own to the grave, and so was dying, not because he needed to, but as one who had the right to offer his death positively, and it was died by one identified with sin-stained men in love to the limit, and with the divine capacity to embrace us all, so it is a death of universal and eternal validity. It was a death which experienced the inexpressible horror of God's implacable determination to destroy sin in sinful man, yet it is God himself who bears the pain of it.

In that death we have an all-sufficient act of atonement, done by God in man's history and man's flesh, for all men at all places and at all times.

Marvellous, but whatever difference can it possbily make when you come down to earth again and are dealing with people like ourselves, with our particular vices, failures and problems. And can it really be said to have made any difference to the history of the world, to the sort of problems our leaders face every day?

Well, let's start near at hand and work out from there.

Jesus' cross and resurrection say the following things to every individual and to the world in general.

First, the cross makes clear what is meant by gospel or good news. The good news is that right in the middle of our history with all its defeats, failures and despairs, and involved to the hilt in them all, God has done a final, divine, perfect, universal deed, has by a death broken the fatal entail of sin and established a new, invulnerable beginning, there in the middle of it all, for all to have. Of course they have to want it for themselves, and while in one sense that's as easy as falling off a log, in another sense the wanting will cost them everything. But when we declare the gospel we are not saying, 'If only you will do this or that, take this step or that step, make up your mind this way or that, God will do his best to come to meet you'. We are saying, 'God *has* broken the hold of evil over the race of man, he has worked the deed of salvation, he has saved you: look round, look up at him, and discover for yourself that it is true'. Gospel tells you about something done independently of you, before you were born, without your consent, without your needing to make any effort about it. A death has been died and a new life provided, here on man's earth. It is yours for the believing.

So, secondly, what is believing? If you are up to your eyes in the consequences of some wrongdoing, what does it mean to believe that Jesus died and rose for your deliverance. What does it mean that he offers you this remedy freely and unconditionally, inviting you only to believe that it is what you need? Well, let us come at this in one or two ways. In the examples I gave at the beginning of this lecture, there were people who knew they were to blame, who were sorry for the fixes they had got themselves into, but who simply couldn't see how they could possibly break the deadlocks they found themselves in. Then in their anguish, they hear Jesus saying, 'I have stood where you stand; I have died the death which you sense as the only escape route, and I am the new chance you are so wildly longing for'. Now probably they will have heard something like those words before, but they have always till now seemed just empty words, maybe a nice-sounding formula, but without any real meaning to them. But now, they find themselves saying, 'Can it be true?', and that movement of the heart in response to Jesus is the beginning of faith but it isn't the whole of faith.

When the boy who is on the edge of the swimming-pool hears his father saying, 'Jump in and I will catch you', faith isn't just believing that in his heart, faith is jumping. So too there is always a practical step towards Jesus that turns the inward beginning of faith into a practical reality. That's why the classical act of Christian faith is baptism, the inward hearing and responding in the heart and the practical going out to the Jesus beyond you. And faith is always made up of those two parts, the inward 'Yes' and the outward step that turns it from a daydream into a fact. Now in the illustrations I gave at the beginning, that step, whatever it is, doesn't look at first sight like changing anything: it doesn't alter your father, it doesn't wash out the consequences of the girl's lying, it doesn't change the hearts of those with the power to blackmail you. What you do find, however, is that because Jesus is real, the weight of the guilt seems to shift and the tensions ease, you have a divine companion with you instead of being so horribly alone, and there always turns out to be a practical step out of the deadlock which you hadn't seen, but which is in fact the way forward to Jesus. Faith means discovering in reality that Jesus has acted and that it does change things.

Thirdly, faith is faith in the Jesus who rose to new life and opened the way to a new chance *through death*. And faith is going to mean, somewhere along the line if not immediately, identification with that Jesus — just as he was identified with us — not only in that new life, but also in that death. So the salvation which he offers is absolutely free, but paradoxically is not cheap, rather it costs everything. And this means that we have to speak of that salvation in two ways. There are some ways of speaking of the death of Christ which makes it sound as if he did everything for us, as it were, over our heads, taking the whole thing quite out of our hands, without our being able to contribute anything to the process and offering us the finished work on a plate. And that is of course quite true. Christ died in our place, because at the crucial point we were too blinded and weakened by our sin to be able to lift hand or foot to make any contribution to our salvation. But if we speak of Christ only as a substitute, we miss part of the glory of the cross, for he is also our representative, doing what he did in us, for us, speaking with our voice, and respecting us enough to offer us a full share in the experience of his own cross, as well as in the triumph of his resurrection. And that is why the step of faith by which we accept Jesus Christ is likely to be a painful one; or if the initial step of faith is not painful, somewhere along the line we shall find we are invited to share the experience whereby he defeated sin through unjust humiliation, pain and death. It is true that he died the only actual death and rose again from the only actual grave, but in believing in him as our Redeemer, we are going in some way or other to know the full glory of new life only through approximating to his dying, so that baptism is spoken of as dying with him. It may be, for example, that we shall have to admit that we did commit the deed that landed us and others in all this trouble, that there were really no extenuating circumstances, that we are, in fact, the mean, nasty person others have been saying we were all along, and that we must stop trying to pretend to a goodness and a reputation we can in fact lay no claim to. It may be there is a humiliating apology to be made to someone who will only receive it with a sneer, asking to know why we have not offered it before. It may be there is a proper act of reparation to be made that will cost us something we did not want to give up, or a penalty to be borne that will rob us of our freedom or cruelly restrict our activity. In one way or another, we shall find, if we are talking about real rather than imaginary sins that the person we have paraded ourselves as has to die, if there is to be a new life in Christ — that new life, whose wonder and freedom we have already had a taste of in our first movement of faith.

Fourthly, as you let this experience of dying and rising with Christ become the central pattern of your spiritual life, you discover that you are catching glimpses of a whole new way of looking not only at yourself but at the end of the world as a whole. It is as if, from the further side of the cross, you are learning falteringly to stand at God's side and see the reality that can only be seen from there. And it is a paradoxical reality.

In regard to yourself, to begin with, you supposed that being saved was going to give you a constant sense of self-approval, that you would now at last feel better about yourself since your sins would be behind you, and that you would be in a strong position to lay down the law to others still in their sins. In fact, as all the saints testify, the more closely you are identified with Christ your Saviour, the more layers of nastiness in yourself you will keep coming across, and the harder it will be to conceive how anyone — let alone Christ — could ever care for you at all — and yet his love for you will be the one great growing, humbling certainty of your life. So the actual process of being made Christ's saint is of feeling it less and less likely that you have ever any hope of being one; of being less and less able to boast of being one of the saved and more and more in sympathy with the situation of the commonest sinner at hand; less ready to censure and condemn others and only too ready to forgive, as you know you live by forgiveness in a community meant for forgiveness; and yet less and less self-occupied with worrying over your failings and more and more eager to keep your gaze fixed on the loving Christ who no doubt is working his will in you, as others may well be aware, even if you are only aware of your grubbiness.

Again, you might have supposed that the victory of the Resurrection was not only the plucking of the sting of death, but also the death-knell on the power of pain and evil to vex us, or at least to vex Christians, whereas the Resurrection seems, instead, to confirm that it is the cross itself that provides the essential way by which the poison of evil is sucked out and all its malignant hurts ultimately healed. This experience of identification with the Crucified does not, I think, provide intellectual answers for the difficulties about the presence of evil in God's world that I talked about last week; but it does strangely seem to transmute the whole problem, so that evil comes to be dissolved at the heart, and begins to serve God's own ends, by that process that the medievals quaintly called 'wounds into worships'.

Make no mistake. There are some evils Christians should fight against by direct frontal assault; there are some pains for which Christian healing powers, in all their range are available and wanting to be used now. But there are some whose hard-core can only be dissolved when someone will take it willingly to himself; some situations where to attack evil will only breed more spite and violence and only the bearing of humiliation and undeserved reproach will pluck the sting. It is only as we learn our way into the experience of the cross, only when, with Lady Julian, we put on the mind of his passion, that we discover at last that evil does not have God's reality, that it is indeed subordinate to him and able to be dissolved out and even contribute to eventual goodness.

It is by standing with Christ at the cross that we begin to learn the mysterious way in which God has provided an answer to the problem of evil and pain.

And fifthly, we look at what it is God gives to the whole world by his cross and resurrection.

The word Saviour, of course, is the same as Liberator. The Jews first came to know that their God had the character of a Saviour because he made them into his own people by liberating them from their oppression in Egypt, and they always knew it was wrong to enslave at any rate their fellow Jews, because they were a race of people set free by God himself. Now it would be hard to describe Jesus as a political leader, but in his concern for the poor and in his willingness to challenge authority, there are overtones which have always rightly given heart to the oppressed and made them see him as their natural champion. In parts of the world like South America and South Africa, where the church has often been too closely identified with oppressive regimes, it is not surprising that many Christians today, siding rather with the victims have developed a theology of liberation which appeals directly to Christ's role as liberator.

It is, however, as they have laboured gravely with others – and the others tend often to be Marxists, left-wingers, members of black-consciousness movements and groups Christians have not always spent a lot of time with – that they have been compelled to identify what is the essential Christian contribution to movements of liberation.

Christ was indeed involved in a public movement which many joined because they sensed it was a layman's movement and would give them freedom from foreign domination.

And it was a sufficiently powerful movement to worry the police, and make the Roman powers ready to help the Jewish authorities to do away with this liberator. But in the crucial encounters, Jesus would have nothing to do with violence, he refused to be manoeuvred into the position where he would have to write off any as his enemies, and in the end, it was he alone, and not a single follower or opponent who bore the only violence his movement led to. And it is this attempt to translate the problem of the cross into the attempts to win more freedom in oppressive regimes that is the distinctive Christian insight into the theories of liberation. Now the cross as a method has often been derided as weakness, has been misunderstood as an unwillingness to contend for justice in this world in favour of waiting for a better deal in a world to come, and has been approached only reluctantly by the more pragmatic liberationists because it is going to involve humiliation used, you might say, almost as a weapon, because it is so hard to recognise what is true cross and what is cowardice, and because to take up the cross requires such faith in God when there is so little evidence one can show to others that God will honour those who trust him. Nevertheless, the Christian's only badge is the cross. Now it ill becomes comfortable property owning Christians like ourselves, who suffer no restrictions on our liberty, to offer advice to or wag fingers at our fellow Christians living under oppression who are tempted to militancy, and side with the violent in the belief that violence is the quickest and fairest way to justice, or to remind them of the way of the cross of which we have little experience here; rather it is they who have the right to speak to us and tell us of a meaning of the word Saviour and of a dimension of the theology of the cross without which we shall not fully understand what a strange and mysterious instrument of healing God has shown us. It is worth recalling that one of the most powerful passages in the New Testament dealing with the inward attitude of the cross is set in the context of what we might call labour relations, and lays upon the oppressed slaves of ancient Rome the charge that there is no situation of injustice where a Christian has any other model to follow than that of Christ in the way he went to his suffering — and thereby worked universal redemption.

And in this very area, and in other areas where men fight for freedom from oppression, for human rights and racial equality and common justice, are there enough of us Christians who are prepared to follow Christ and both find themselves quite unashamed to be part of against-the-stream liberation movements, yet also to set themselves to make the cross their badge and pattern, refusing to sneer-down any as their enemies, refusing to settle for violence, except, if necessary, to themselves, trusting that obedience to God all the way to some Calvary in the end brings the largest freedom.

The cross as a pattern is a mixture of worldliness and unworldliness which it is very hard to learn — and maybe it is learned through practising in small ways first — even just in relation to people which whom we live or work who also irritate us.

But it is at the cross that we are brought to the heart of God, that we learn that there is nothing that can outlast or overcome crucified love; and it is as we learn to be people of the cross that the world discovers with relief the paradoxical almightiness of God.

Before Jesus lived among us and died on his cross, mankind did not know if truly God was the final power in the universe, and we did not know if the virtues of love, compassion, forgiveness, had any basis in the grain of the world. Since that stark, terrible, lonely day on Calvary, and its Easter-morning vindication, we do know the answer to these questions, and God himself has shown us, for our redemption and creation's restoring, and has put into our hands to make that redemption an ever-continuing reality, this strange, marvellous instrument of healing, his cross for the world's blessing.

It is an extraordinary thing that after the meteoric appearance of Jesus among men, his followers didn't spend their time looking back nostalgically to the good old days of his earthly life. If anything, they appear to be looking forward, expectantly standing on their toes, necks craned forward looking to the final fulfilment of what he set in motion; and meanwhile living with an expanded joy and excitement, experiencing Jesus as more present, if that was possible, than ever before.

If you contrast this with other idealistic movements, you begin to see the distinctiveness of the Church's experience. Other movements, in the light of some great discovery, some new teaching, some fresh insight, some new political theory, burst forth upon the world for a period, until the first flush of enthusiasm wanes, and then there is the looking back to the source and spring of it all, the anxious investigations of the theorists to see if they are being faithful to the original deposit, the gradual realisation that what was once true no longer really applies to today, the gradual transformation, the abandonment of the original name of the movement and so on. Or sometimes a movement will start off with high ideals and then will gradually permit itself such tyrannical acts to enforce compliance on others that it discredits itself out of existence. Or sometimes a movement will simply run out of steam. In these varying accounts you can hear echoes of how the Christian Church has been tempted to behave on and off throughout its chequered history. Yet it continues to find the Jesus of 2,000 years ago not only normative, but present and inspiring, indeed the heart of its inner life, and in spite of betrayals and terrible wickedness committed sometimes in the very name of God himself, continues to be renewed, reformed, to produce saints, to influence society, to gain credibility and immediate understanding among people and cultures to the very ends of the earth, to make the name of Jesus known and beloved in every language and to make his gospel a practical possibility for living in generation after generation.

We are speaking about the Holy Spirit.

When we speak of the Holy Spirit, essentially what we mean is God, God focused in the experience of men as Jesus Christ, God making the experience of that Jesus universal and present in the hearts of men everywhere, God building up into a supernatural, worldwide family those who by sacramental faith have committed themselves to Jesus, God continuing his purpose through that family.

It was always the intention of the Holy God to dwell fully among men. Jesus was the evidence that he could do so, and Jesus is the means by which we wonderful but wounded men can in fact become the temple of the Holy God. The Holy Spirit brings all that Jesusness of God within the experience of the hearts of men, and makes them aware of the family likeness to Jesus and now to one another. Of course there is a work of the Holy Spirit outside the Church, trying to draw men's attention to Christ, trying to gain entrance for him into hearts and lives and situations, breathing God's life into idealism and goodness everywhere and trying to help it find focus and permanence in Jesus. But the fullest work of the Holy Spirit is among those whose eyes he has in fact opened to Jesus. Among them, you might say, the Holy Spirit works divinity unrestricted. He works in them the *experience* of God through Jesus Christ; he produces in them the *character* of God as we saw it in Jesus Christ; he uses them to forward the *purpose* of God as Jesus Christ enacted it.

He does this primarily, I suppose, among the *fellowship* of believers, so that the Church is properly called the fellowship of the Holy Spirit and is his work; but he does it also, as far as is possible, among individual Christians, so that he is the maker of saints. Because he is God's *love*, he has made them into a new sort of fellowship, that can take its shape in any culture and century, that, in spite of faults, has an astonishing capacity for survival and renewal, that has made love the primary virtue wherever the gospel has been accepted, that is always discovering new shapes of community in which to explore the riches of this love of God more deeply, that has developed a spirituality not of self-realisation but of adoration and love overflowing into fascination with all men.

Because he is God's *power*, he has been able, through the Church, to convict men of sin and bring them truly to their knees, to heal sick and broken-hearted, to break deadlocks that have defied all human ingenuity, to mend those who have been long and deeply damaged, and to convert hopeless failures into new people, and to give mortals a heady taste of the experience of God.

Because he is God's *wisdom* he has continually helped the Church to see its way to truth — both for itself, in the working out of a coherent theology, and for the world by providing a true criterion of understanding how to discern God's guidance and his hand in prophecy, and he has helped individuals to see God's pattern for their lives and has opened their ears to special callings.

Because he is the *holiness* of God, he has shaped a Christlike conscience in the Church, has made saints out of sinners, has altered the standard of the world's morality and has helped us all to see what is true humanity.

And since, in all this and with all this he is above all the *Spirit of Jesus*, he continues to focus men's attention on Jesus as the standard and test of all things, *the historical Jesus*, that man who was the only demonstration of God we have seen that does not arise from our own minds, the *Jesus of faith* and present experience working himself out in every culture and every Christian's heart. When St. John gave as the true test of spiritual experience the dictum 'every spirit that does not confess Jesus Christ come in the flesh is not of God' he is speaking sternly in the midst of a multiplicity of deceptive spiritual experiences, but he has rightly understood the nature of the Holy Spirit — he is God in our midst *through Jesus Christ*.

But alas for the paradox:

The Holy Spirit is the totality of God as declared in Jesus, the totality of God willing now to abide in fullness among men whose one qualification is that they accept and know that they are nothing but sinners who live only by the grace of the Saviour. And because Christians are, *by definition*, fallible sinners, listening to the Holy Spirit with dirty ears, welcoming him into grubby hearts, trying to understand him with limited minds, starting out on the road to holiness with such a baggage of prejudices and inborn disabilities, even making up Jesus for themselves out of their own presuppositions, so every one of the glorious claims I have made for the work of the Holy Spirit in his Church can be matched by its opposite and negation.

The fellowship of love — known for its divisions and its mutual suspicions.

The fellowship of power — known for its apathy, or for power misused.

The fellowship of wisdom — known for its belated blindness.

The fellowship of holiness — known for its thin, colourless virtues and its cranks.

The fellowship of Jesus, that has so often succeeded in disguising his real explosiveness.

Or again, because the Holy Spirit is the totality of God wanting to dwell among such limited men as Christians are, so we have picked the bits of his grace that come congenially to us and been blind to the others, we have gone for the exercise of spiritual power at the expense of love and wisdom, we have gone for wisdom in ways that quite missed out on holiness, we have gone for a holiness that did not always look like Jesus and that forgot about love, we have gone for thin charities that shied away from power, and have altogether been inadequate to welcome and represent the fullness of the divine Jesus whose body we claim we are.

And God the Holy Spirit makes do with us and never gives up on us, and is content to go on trusting that he can say God to the world through us, over the top of us, in spite of us, by means of us when we are least conscious of him, but always in relation to us.

No Christian can speak without deep shame of the Church, but to speak truly we must speak primarily of its glory, humbly, penitently loving and trusting it because God continues to do so, entrusting his divinity to it, never despairing of it, constantly bringing it out of its winters into his spring, content to employ no other body to speak himself to men.

So I come to talk about the Church, which I have called The Travelling Company. I have called it that to stress that it is both a close-knit association of friends who know one another well, and also that it is not a static corporation but a movement on the march. There are many other ways of speaking about the Church, and I want to examine some of them now, but I believe these two elements of close relationship and movement should be born in mind as touchstones all the way along.

Jesus himself seems hardly to have spoken of the Church as a recognisable structure but, of course, he knew what it was to be a member of the chosen people, and as the very first disciples did, he set about gathering a group round him to express what he saw God's Israel to mean. So the underside of Jesus' ministry is really the training of that group. And a very odd group it was: It included what looks like one southerner in a group predominantly of northerners; one member of a group wedded to the idea of driving out the Roman occupier by force, and another who collected taxes for them; one man full of doubts and others ready to call down fire from heaven on a village that was a bit slow to believe in Jesus; some who pushed themselves forward, and others who no doubt got pushed to the back. And he gave them no opportunity to discuss one another's suitability for his company, but gave them to one another, took them all completely into his confidence and shared everything he was doing with them.

And it became an extraordinary story of stumbling forward into a relationship of quite unforeseen depth, which was finally crystallised and supernaturalised by the sacramental gift of the body and blood of his new covenant death, and by the gift of his own Spirit. Before, therefore, the Church came to be thought of as a structure and defined in structural terms, it was known first as an *experience*, and it is vitally important that this should always be remembered. The experience had four elements to it, the presence of Jesus at its heart, the *sacred* character of the relationship between members, the knowledge that it was a task-fellowship, and the feeling of being a pilgrim band, one foot in this world and one already in the world of the task completed. Before we get to the word 'church' then, and long before we think of the church as nave altars, class meetings, archdeacons, Councils of Trent, apostolic succession, parish registers, liturgical revision, and redundant buildings, there is an experience for which the word 'Church' is the only possible description, and from the start men and women discovered that there is no way of being a Christian except by entering into this experience.

Because of the nature of the experience, however, it is possible to describe the Church in terms of the inward quality of the experience and the form required to express it, or in terms of the Church's task, and particularly in relation to those outside its membership, or in ways which use the world's terms and describe it as one particular sort of corporate body among all those others to be found in human society.

As examples of the first way, we may glance at the terms 'the fellowship of the Holy Spirit' and 'the body of Christ'.

The phrase 'the fellowship of the Holy Spirit' shows no interest in shape or structure, in continuity, hierarchy or meeting-places. It expresses above all the sheer intoxicated delight of knowing Jesus alive in the midst through the Spirit, it dwells on the love he pours out in us when our eyes begin to open to one another. (Do you remember Paul's striking words: 'Concerning love of the brethren, you have no need that I should write to you'?) It lives with gratitude that we can go on being forgiven into holiness; it rejoices to discover that God has actually allowed us to use his own supernatural powers to do his work, and make us new people in the process, discovering in ourselves talents we never knew we had; it finds with wonder that it is a body maturing in wisdom to deal with problems from without and eccentricities within; it learns slowly but surely that there is a path of prayer and worship to take it ever deeper into God. Of course, this way of speaking of the church by itself can lead to distortion, to exaggerated attachment to spiritual fizzpop, to silly prancings followed by ignominious flops on the face, to censoriousness towards those with less to show in the spiritual window, to an obsession with a spirituality of glory and a stunted spirituality of the cross, to an emphasis on spiritual phenomena and a forgetting of Christ's poor in the world. Yes, heads must be hung in shame here, but when we speak of the church as the fellowship of the Holy Spirit, we are saying with fervent happiness that God is to be experienced in the Church with joy and wonder and power.

The phrase 'the body of Christ' attempts to define this inward experience more vividly and sharply, but it is also concerned with the form that the experience required in order to express itself, and perhaps it further takes notice of what the church looks like to an outsider in that the phrase 'body of Christ' implies that the Church is in some way meant to look like Jesus and convey the same impression that he conveyed.

The description is very striking because of the organically integrated quality of the relationship between the members that it implies, as compared with all other models of corporate organisation. In most forms of corporate organisation the members are, first, self-subsistent independent individuals who, secondly, opt to join and work together in some form of association. In a body, the members are first functions of or parts of the shape of the body, and only secondly have separate independent names. No member has any independent life in itself, since life is a function of the body, and any member cut off from the body simply withers and dies. The diversity of the body only adds to its complex efficiency, and no member can think of itself as the one essential; so close is the organic interconnection of all the members, that if you hurt your foot, you feel sick in your stomach, or conversely, if your mind is free of anxiety, you eat better and you pray better.

Now, even if we accept that the phrase 'the body of Christ' is a metaphor, it clearly is trying to find a way of expressing a depth of interdependence, of mutual belonging, of inseparability, of subordination of the individual member to a greater, supernatural whole, which takes it beyond a merely voluntary human association into a mystical organism. The very phrase, linking the Church with the work of Christ on the cross where his body was broken and his blood shed, and with the sacrament of Holy Communion, where that — once for all — work of redemption is made a continually renewed reality in us, points to the source of that supernatural, unifying experience. Because there is one loaf, we, many as we are, are one body, because we all share in the one loaf.

Clearly this image of the body of Christ drives us very deeply into the understanding of our unity together in Christ. Clearly it does compel us to ask about the actual shape and form and activity of the Church, to see whether it does, in fact, picture Christ, does convey the feel of him, does do what he does, and in the way that he did it.

Clearly, it can be used to make very sharp definitions both of the form of the body and of what ensures membership, and this is both important and also can be dangerous in a fellowship where sometimes one also wants to argue for fuzzy edges rather than for too black and white distinction between who is and who is not a member.

But, in general, the phrase 'the body of Christ' provides the most fertile soil of any of the images used for the devotional exploration of the nature of the Church's life. In addition to the traditional religious communities, with all their wealth of committed, corporate experience, there are today a whole range of newer Christian communities which, from one angle and another, emphasising one aspect of truth or another, trying some of them to get away from the single-sex life-vow communities to communities of more mixed membership, aiming to fulfil one side of Christian work or another, are an attempt to discover, as experimental stations on behalf of the whole Church, more about the depths to which Christ wants to take us in the supernaturally corporate experience of being his body, and to see how much of this specialist experience can be translated into the life of ordinary Christian congregations all over the world as part of their essential life.

It is somewhat more difficult to get a suitable-for-all-seasons description of the Church in its relationship to the world around, and it is in this area that most of the rude adjectives in relation to the Church are found — quietist, triumphalist, proselytising, compromising, ineffective, worldly. The contrasts here suggest that in different eras and different circumstances the Church has to adjust its relation to the world, and does not always find it easy to do so, or is slow off the mark.

Jesus' own models of salt and leaven, however, at once make clear that the Church is not a body that can be adequately defined simply in relation to itself. You won't think much of the man who invited you to supper and gives you only a plateful of salt, and no housewife supposes that you can make anything at all just out of yeast. Salt is of no use, indeed it is unpleasant, unless it is in some other ingredients to flavour them, and the essential use of yeast is to be put into the dough to make it rise. If we follow this way of thinking, the Church is of no use, and indeed cannot be defined, on its own. Its nature can only be seen when it is in the world to flavour it and bring it to the height of its potential. (One is reminded here of the less-than-Biblical comment on the clergy who are sometimes said to be like manure — spread thinly over the land they do an awful lot of good; brought together in a heap by themselves, they . . . well you can guess the run of the saying!)

Essentially, however, Jesus appears to be saying that for all its greatness the church is not a final form in itself. In St. John 17, he says that the Church is in the world but not of it — once again a stance not easy to discover, certainly not to maintain. A more moving statement of the ideal is found in a second century letter written to an unknown friend called the epistle to Diognetus.

Here is an extract:

'For Christians are not distinguished from the rest of mankind either in locality or in speech or in customs. For they dwell not somewhere in cities of their own, neither do they use some different language, nor practise an extraordinary kind of life. Nor again do they possess any invention discovered by any intelligence or study of ingenious men, nor are they masters of any human dogma as some are. But while they dwell in cities of Greeks and barbarians as the lot of each is cast, and follow the native customs in dress and food and the other arrangements of life, yet the constitution of their own citizenship, which they set forth, is marvellous, and confessedly contradicts expectation. They dwell in their own countries, but only as sojourners; they bear their share in all things as citizens and they endure all hardships as strangers. Every foreign country is a fatherland to them, and every fatherland is foreign. They marry like all other men and they beget children; but they do not cast away their offspring. They have their meals in common, but not their wives. They find themselves in the flesh, and yet they live not after the flesh. Their existence is on earth, but their citizenship is in heaven. They obey the established laws, and they surpass the laws in their own lives. They love all men, and they are persecuted by all. Doing good they are punished as evil-doers; being punished they rejoice, as if they were thereby quickened by life. War is waged against them as aliens by the Jews, and persecution is carried on against them by the Greeks, and yet those that hate them cannot tell the reason of their hostility.

'In a word, what the soul is in a body, this the Christians are in the world.'

Now this author wrote at a time when Christians had, as it were, only a toehold in the world, and so were not yet under the temptation of becoming a worldly body. But when, in accordance with the gospel command to preach Christ to all men, they finally overcame the hostility of the world and became the accepted religion of the civilised earth, then it became harder and harder to maintain the position of not being of the world. On the contrary, when the church had won the position of being accepted as the conscience of society, it has tended to become a force for conservatism, a strong defender of the old values, repeatedly lumped with the establishment, looking askance at words like radical and revolutionary which, one might have thought, more nearly describe its essential dynamic nature. And here one sees what a paradoxical body the Church is. It is its work and its glory to be able to make the gospel of Jesus Christ native in any culture, time and place, so that Christianity properly wears every people's dress and speaks every nation's language. But as soon as it becomes incarnate and absorbed in any civilisation, it begins to betray its own nature, and must be listening for God's voice telling it to up sticks and move on.

Perhaps the best way of understanding the provisionality of the Church, though no doubt the hardest for all who bear office in her, is to recognise that Church is essentially an intermediate term, of which the fulfilment is not Church but Kingdom. If the Church was to carry out its apostolic mission so effectively that everyone everywhere were to be converted tonight, and were to become fully paid up, active, worshipping, loving church members, God's purpose would not be fulfilled. The Church is meant to point on to that purpose, it is the instrument for fulfilling that purpose to which he has most completely committed himself, its life is meant to give the best possible foretaste of what that purpose fulfilled might be, and the greatest spur to realising it, but it is not itself the fulfilment. As a divine assembly of sinful men, it must itself stand under the final judgement, before God can draw back the curtain on his own ultimate work, the Kingdom. So, we are reminded that by nature the

Church is intended to be not a static body but a dynamic one, not a great institution venerated by all, but a pilgrim band often out of step with the world, not simply the world with its religious make-up on, but a movement, a challenge, a pricking conscience, a crusade, a travelling company living in tents without settled territory till Kingdom come. How hard to maintain this tension; and the parish churches of this country, dotted up and down the East Riding in such beauty and profusion, are the classic illustration of it. Those churches were built because with years of simple preaching, loving and ministering, the hearts of English villagers were won by Christ, they put their old ways behind them, they took on the yoke of the gospel and lifted up their hearts in song and stone to adore him who had brought them to the glory of this new life. For us their successors, grateful as we are for this marvellous heritage, they are often an economic burden, a hindrance to fresh thinking, an identification of the church with what is ancient, a localizing and tying of us to an old style of living out the life of Christ. As its life goes forward, the Church always will and must live with this contradiction. By the power of Christ, it will capture the heart of a culture and come to express his life in terms of the best fruits of its civilisation, only to find itself caught on the wrong foot as life moves inexorably forward and it now is lumped into a past age, while its best sons irritate it with rude remarks and set out to win the heart of the next generation and the new pop culture.

We are perhaps only too familiar with the picture of the Church as an institution among the other institutions of the world to need to labour the point here, except perhaps to say that I suppose our generation is more embarrassed than some have been over the word 'Institution', for the account does not all come out on the negative side. And even where as an institution the Church has been at its most pompous and its most worldly we can sometimes catch the echo of God laughing in the wings and doing his own real work covertly behind the bitter facade.

I suppose the temptation to become an Institution arises as the very penalty of success. At the heart of its organised life are three constants, the sacraments, the scriptures and the ordained ministry. As the numbers of the faithful grow, each of these gathers to itself a great superstructure that seems to link it more and more closely with the institutions of the world.

As worshippers gather in greater and greater numbers round the sacraments, the Church becomes the owner of great shrines, and needs to provide for their maintenance. As the study of the Scriptures goes deeper, institutions of higher learning proliferate with armies of theologians, canon lawyers and even a holy office to keep a check on freer thinkers. And those called by God to give up everything to minister full-time in the service of the Church become a hierarchy of such power as to provide David Edwards' remark that of all the great religions of the world, Christianity is the most heavily clericalised.

To look over the story of this great historical institution, the Church, is to behold much splendour, because in it the glory of God and the best of man are affirmed; but it is also to behold too much human pride, too great a desire to outrival all other institutions out of a false concern for God's pre-eminence.

And yet, in, with and under it all, God has nevertheless continued to work his own truly important work, in the hearts and lives of ordinary people, in the softening of the cruelty of the oppressors, in the gentling of the style of human living, in the blossoming of saints in every sort of soil.

But I should like to devote the remaining part of this lecture to a more thorough examination of one classic statement of the nature of the Church in the Christian creeds: I believe in one Holy Catholic Apostolic Church.

One holy, catholic, apostolic church — this great affirmation that in one's more cynical moments seems to fly in the face of every bit of the evidence. But I shall not forget that when one talks of the Church, one talks also of the Holy Spirit, who is its life, and so one talks reverently and looking for the inward truth that makes the Church a beacon of hope in a sometimes rudderless world.

I believe in one Church — which one? How in the world is one to be persuaded that the statement means anything at all? Christians, God forgive us, commanded to love one another, told that it is by our unity that Christ will be recognised by the world as the one sent by God, we are more commonly known for our divisiveness, for our inability to trust one another, for our excommunication and disowning of one another, for our claim to love one another provided we can keep one another at arms' length and agree to do nothing significant together. It is a tragedy that words like sect, heresy, denomination are specifically Christian words, coined to describe something that was never intended to exist. It is a tragedy that if a man arriving on earth asked if he could be put in touch with the Church, he could receive no straightforward answer: he could be told where to find the Methodist Church or the Church of the Latter Day Saints or the Church of Christ, Scientist, but he could not be pointed to one body that everyone agreed was just — the Church. How can anyone say he believes in one Church?

There are two wrong answers both with enough right in them to point to the true answer.

First, there are those who say that the idea of a visible unity of the Church is a will-o'-the-wisp, an unspiritual attempt to produce an organisational monolith, that Christ has no interest in such a thing, and that in any case there is no hope of its ever coming true. But there *is* an invisible unity of all true believers, who in every denomination recognise one another, share an experience of Christ's saving love, have a sense of brotherhood and who are already one in the Spirit. What is to be made of this notion of spiritual oneness? Certainly it is not something the world can see, and so it can hardly demonstrate Christ's lordship publicly; it appears to be so spiritual as to preclude the likelihood of practical action together; and it has sometimes an oddly sectarian flavour about it. This sense of spiritual unity which fears to risk itself in visible, practical action is not what is meant by One Church. But insofar as there is here an instinctive feeling that the heart of the Church's unity is a deep, spiritual mutual trust, a supernatural love that can transcend barriers of background and temperament, a sense of common brotherhood, an instinctive recognition of one's fellows in Christ whatever the colour of their skins, the language they use and the ceremonies they go for, then this view is true. The most ardent crusader for organisational unity takes it for granted, and so probably does not make it clear enough, that real love and trust, rooted in the grace of

Christ himself, are the only significant heart-meaning of the Church's unity.

Secondly, particular churches have sometimes said, 'I believe in one Church — and we are it'. Before the Second Vatican Council, the Roman Catholic Church in the west affirmed with a straightforward confidence that they were the one true church and that to be outside the communion of truth that they represented, to be out of fellowship with the Holy Father in Rome was quite simply to be outside the Church. There could be no recognition of others as Christians, let alone churches, no admission that others' sacraments were effective means of unifying and sanctifying grace. Whatever graces were to be found outside the Roman Church were uncovenanted mercies, rub-offs from the abounding grace overflowing from the true Church, and they should not delude anyone into supposing that they implied anything more than this. Now the strength of the argument for this meaning of the Church's unity is its straightforward self-evident simplicity — one church here means one church, plain for all to see; and when it is in fact in many areas in the west the most widespread and the largest of the Christian churches, it is not difficult to argue that other Christian bodies are but fragments from the one true church, who could, if they really cared for Christian unity, quite simply repent and return to the true fold.

However, the Roman Church was never able to maintain this view with complete consistency. It was aware that in the east were the Orthodox Churches which had preserved all those marks which the Roman Church claimed were the marks of the true Church, and it found itself unable to declare with any hope of conviction that the Orthodox Churches were not churches. And if it was possible to admit that bodies not in communion with the Pope were churches, what became of the claim to be the one Church? Again, as relations between Christians in the west became closer, less controversial and more open to humble exchange of views and experiences, it became evident that it was not only sin in the separating churches but sin also in the Roman Church which had been a factor in disunity; and there was a willingness to admit that some aspects of Christian truth that had become obscured in Roman Christianity had been preserved for the whole church by those who had separated. So while the old Roman conviction that to speak of one Church means to be able to point to one definable, joinable, visibly and organisationally united body with its officers, its symbols and its sacraments open for all the world to see, *remains a true one*, the Second Vatican Council recognised that simply to say that they and they alone fulfilled Christian intention, was insufficient, that there was a larger unity yet to come, that must be discovered by penitence and prayer, patient discussion and serious study, by steps towards mutual recognition and a gradual edging towards a oneness we can hardly yet conceive of, within the limitless love of Christ.

And that points on to what I take to be the true meaning of the phrase, I believe in One Church. It must surely mean, I believe, that it was the intention of Christ that there should only be one church — I will never settle for anything less; I will live, work and pray in the constant expectation that even out of our sinfulness and blindness, Christ's will can be done and that we can look to the dawning of the day when we shall wake up and find we are all plainly members of the One Church, visible to all the world, and that there is no other. That belief needs a bit of filling out. First, it is a spiritual thing.

Christians say they have divided because they held irreconcilable views which they claimed they could not compromise with, but it is a sad fact of experience more than belief, that it was the sinful temperamental irritation between the believers that eventually divided them — and Christ said, 'If you love those who love you, what reward have you; do not even the publicans do the same?' It does not need the grace of God to hold together those who already get on easily enough. The divine, miraculous grace and love of God is seen where it holds and binds together those who use words and sing things and go in for customs and follow fashions that naturally irritate, exasperate or dismay one another. Where people love one another, where they take it for granted that they are blood-members of one family, they can live with some differences, they can work their way towards better understandings of truths which have divided them, for there is, as a simple fact, no way of arriving at full Christian truth in disunity. Wherever Christians have parted over belief, each side has finished with a thinner or distorted or out-of-context version of the truth contended for, for love itself is an essential part of truth. Secondly, it is probable that a united Church will not be a uniform monolith. A Church with love accepted as the unbreakable heart of its life will tolerate different styles, will rejoice in different local customs, will baptise different cultural expressions, will accept that it may not fully have comprehended some aspect of the truth and can therefore tolerate some variety of emphasis on the way to a consensus, and so it will hesitate to expel members who can't help being, maybe like being, exceptions to the norm on the way to our ultimate arriving at the many-splendoured wisdom of God. But while one Church will be a great advertisement for that diversity that God himself loves, it will nevertheless be visibly one in the sense that it will have a common jurisdiction, a recognised membership — even if with fluffy edges — will partake in one sacrament of Christ's body and blood, will be able to speak with one voice, preach one gospel and so point unmistakably to the one God and Saviour.

For the present, it seems to me that we must be aware of God's Spirit strongly at work among us to bring us back to unity, and must try to follow where he leads. There are rhythms, hiccoughs, advances and setbacks on the road to unity; there are sudden visions and breakthroughs, and then shudderings as we realise what unity will cost to old securities. But there must be no succumbing to cynicism, no giving up of hope, no mocking of those who make proposals. I remember a saintly old man, strongly opposed on conscientious grounds to a particular unity scheme appearing on a platform one day and saying, 'I read in my devotions this morning the words "If thou art offering thy gift at the altar and there rememberest that thy brother hath ought against thee, leave there thy gift, first be reconciled to thy brother and then come and offer thy gift", so I have decided to change my vote'. It is chiefly by penitence that unity is won.

The phrase, I believe in one holy Church need perhaps occupy us for less time. Once again, to call the church holy will often seem a mockery. A Church that has burnt heretics, and has been blind to crying social evils, a Church called the Church of the Redeemer that has again and again been found on the side of the oppressor, a Church that has taken the great Christian virtues and trivialised them into drawing-room conventions, how can such a Church be called holy?

Let us thank God that when we say we believe that Church is holy we do not mean that Christians are holier than their neighbours, though, by God, they ought to be. (It is worth saying that to many an outsider, the first sign of holiness is the actual admission by Christians that they have done wrong, that they do make mistakes, that they do not have all the answers, that they are willing to admit before men that they are the sinners they say they are to God.) To say that the Church is holy means quite simply that Christ has committed himself to it for ever, that he will never desert it, that sin as it may, he will reform it, split as it may be he will work to re-unite it, sink into apathy as it may, he will revive it by his Spirit, accommodate itself to the world as it may, he will shame it into freshness with his great passionate pageant of saints born in its midst.

Though the Church will again and again look like an assembly of fallible, posturing men, though from time to time one may be reduced almost to despair by its trivialities, its sinfully blind concern simply with its own affairs, this is never the whole truth about it. The anchoring truth is that God loves it: and the gifts and calling of God are irrevocable, and that therefore he will not let it fail. It may fail here or there, it may even die here or there through inanition or sin, but he will raise it up again to be his gospel instrument to the world. And to say, 'I believe in the holy Church', means that I have so learned to trust that God loves the Church that I will never under any circumstances leave it or suppose I can make up its equivalent on my own. Sometimes the atmosphere in church gets so dogged with irrelevancies that you feel the only way to breathe a pure air and to make fresh contact with God is to cut the painter and leave it. Well, maybe we do need holidays from ecclesiasticism, but the grace of God, the hope of redemption, the power of renewal, the ultimate healing of our wounds are to be found nowhere else but in the holy Church.

When we say, 'I believe in one, holy, catholic Church', we are affirming, since catholic means universal, that we belong to a Church that is native in every part of the world. When the Holy Spirit of Pentecost spoke the wonderful works of God in the multitudinous languages of mankind, he was owning every culture as suitable for the reception of Christ as their own Lord and Saviour. When we speak of the catholic Church, we mean that, while in some sense the Christ of Nigeria is a Nigerian Christ and the Christ of South Africa is a South African Christ, incarnate up to the hilt in South African problems, nevertheless the Christians of all those different parts at once recognise one another as belonging to the same family, a family whose claims must sometimes transcend the claims of their own nation and their own national church.

And so perhaps the word catholic is used most obviously to describe a spirit, a temper, and again the sinfulness of the Church is seen in the fact that we can best understand the catholic temper by contrasting it with the protestant spirit. Protestantism represents that great, vigourous, personal spirit of protest against every sort of corruption that so easily inheres in a great sacred institution that sees itself as beyond human criticism. It is that instinctive spirit of freedom that appeals over the head of officialdom and hierarchical authority directly to God himself, and insists rightly that every individual has a direct and immediate line of access to the throne of grace. Sadly, though, this is not implicit in the spirit of protestantism; the protestant tends to be defined as one who in the last resort prefers his own judgement of God's will to the judgement of the Church. The catholic will be as ready as any protestant to call the Church constantly to reform itself, but will stop short of finally disowning its authority or turning his back on it. for the true catholic will ultimately distrust himself, and will agonisingly accept that the Church is indeed holy, and that even if its eyes are blind, as it seems, to truth now, God will bring it back to a fuller and better truth than any separatory individual can. It is lovely and hopeful, of course, that the terms catholic and protestant often cross the floor of the house; some Christians who would bear the name of protestant with great pride would be the last people on earth ever to rebel against or leave the Church, whereas *some* of those who like to call themselves catholic and appeal to the sense of the true church, mean by that phrase some church of their own conceiving, which agrees with their particular views and not the one they are actually in. In general however, we use the word catholic to describe that Christian temper that holds the church itself in high regard and honour, whatever its faults. And with this spirit of reverence for the Church goes a catholic spirituality that draws on the resources of the catholic centuries and the experience of the monasteries and which is available to all. In short, to say 'I believe in the catholic Church' is usually an expression of reverent admiration of the church our mother, a setting aside of private judgement in deference to its long historical wisdom and experience, a devout trust in its essential and universal rootedness in God.

The affirmation, 'I believe in the Apostolic Church', declares at once that the Church of the apostles, the Church standing nearest to the incarnate Christ himself, is normative for the Church throughout its history. For though the Church trusts in the ever-fresh guidance of the Holy Spirit to help it to face issues not envisaged in apostolic times, it takes for granted that the Holy Spirit points always to Jesus and guides in accordance with what God showed himself actually to be like in the Incarnation, and what he actually created in the apostolic Church.

To express belief in the apostolic Church has three implications.

First, it implies that the Church teaches the faith that was taught by the apostles — and this is taken essentially to mean now that it teaches the faith which is rooted in the scriptures. For the apostles, the Bible by which they interpreted the great event of Jesus was the Old Testament, and with this as guide, they set down in pastoral letters, in gospels and in other writings what they made of Jesus, what he taught and what this all implied, writings which for their faithfulness to the incarnate Jesus came to be fixed in time as the New Testament and accepted as authoritative. It is well enough known that Christians have quarrelled over almost everything in scripture, have claimed scripture's authority to disagree with scripture, have *sometimes* set human reason above scripture and at *others* have quite abandoned human reason in blind adherence to the word of scripture. But if we try to follow Jesus' own attitude to scripture, it looks as if he felt himself to be deeply under the authority of scripture as the place where he expected to find God's will shown to him, but along with this attitude of respect he seems to have displayed a quite astonishing freedom in order to allow scripture to speak God's *living* word. Accepting that his is a quite special case, in that it is he whom above every written page we call the Word of God, we nevertheless try to follow that attitude, whereby we bring the insights of a reason enlightened by the Holy Spirit and the experience of other Christians and experts to an understanding of scripture, but acknowledge ourselves to be under its authority and not judge over it. The Bible, understood with the help of the living tradition, remains the normative authority for the apostolic Church.

Secondly, the phrase means that the church today maintains a personal continuity with the Church of the apostles, and so is the same Church not only by teaching but by historical human descent, and this is what is meant in essence by the emotive phrase apostolic succession. In the second century when there was a tendency for Christians to do what was right in their own eyes, and to claim secret apostolic authority for their own pet fancies, the Church came to accept three norms to define its catholicity — the canon of the New Testament, the Rule of Faith, that is, the Creed arising from the threefold answers to the baptismal questions, and the open succession of bishops in their sees. Apostolic succession as a literal theory fails at a vital point, in that it is not possible to show that any of the earliest bishops whose names we know was consecrated by any of the twelve or by St. Paul, but the general claim that the second century Church could show that it loyally remained the Church that the apostles had founded, and that it intended through its officers to maintain this continuity, was sound, and in fact, however the succession is ensured today, almost all the Christian Churches do recognise continuity with the Church of the apostles as essential, and do make some attempt to ensure it through the way their leaders are called and appointed. Clearly when the Church is trying to discover its way home to unity again, the position and significance accorded to these leaders is going to be argued about —

since while it is not unreasonable to claim that the oldest and longest-standing means of ensuring continuity, that is, through bishops, is the true one, it is also true that as a historical fact, bishops have often been those who have most firmly resisted attempts to recover for the church aspects of apostolic truth that have been obscured — but the essential principle that the Church does not just happen afresh in each place and each generation by the work of the Holy Spirit *from scratch*, but preserves and values its continuity with the apostles by a succession of authorised persons would be generally accepted.

And thirdly, the phrase, 'the apostolic Church' means exactly what it says, the missionary Church, just as the Church of the apostles was a missionary Church; and here we are brought again back from a consideration of the Church's internal structure to its function in the world. William Temple spoke powerfully of the apostolic church when he described it as the one society which exists for the sake of those who are not its members. The Church, when it is true to its apostolic nature, takes Christ's good news to the ends of the earth, cares for his poor and oppressed wherever they are found, heals those longing for his redemption, remains, not an institution but a movement, working in every corner of the world but not committed to it, and expects the Holy Spirit to extend it cell-wise in every nation and stratum of life under the sun, One Holy Catholic Apostolic Church. And perhaps we ought not to spend time arguing about apostolic succession, except in intervals to draw breath in the course of working together with apostolic energy.

Anyone speaking of the Church as I have tonight must speak both of its glory and its shame. There can be no disguising of the errors and the scandals, the quarrels and the wickedness that stain its history from first to last, for it is a company of sinners, sinners who are experiencing salvation, but sinners; and those who love the Church most and are most loyal to it, blush deepest for its disgrace, and though they will not sneer at nor dissociate themselves from it, they will often break their hearts over its awfulness.

But they also know its glories, watch people healed, changed and maximised in its fellowship, see it performing fine brave and useful acts of service, sometimes more unconsciously than deliberately, recognise that it has continually helped to form the conscience of mankind and to civilise the society of men, humbly take off their hats to its saints and martyrs, and know that it is here and here alone that a man can come to Christ in the hope of growing up truly into him, and they love it.

Very humbly, but very proudly I say, I believe in One Holy Catholic and Apostolic Church.

Under the Holy Spirit those eleven men and their successors exist to make Christ and his work contemporary and available to everyone.

Reflecting God's Nature

It might fairly be said that Christianity is a combination of believing, belonging and doing. The doing part is particularly congenial to the English temperament, and many a bluff Englishman would once have been happy enough to define a Christian as an honest, good chap, who behaves decently in his own home, who would help a lame dog over a stile, and who would not willingly cause anyone any harm. If pressed, he might go so far as to accept in the way of guidance the Ten Commandments and the Sermon on the Mount, in the fond conviction that these are easy to keep. Generally speaking, there is little doubt that if a religion does not produce some practical fruits in conduct, it will be hard put to it to justify itself on other grounds, but it is becoming increasingly clear, or so it seems to me, that morality does not support itself, but grows out of more fundamental convictions and beliefs. It is interesting, for instance, that a learned Hindu, in a religion where God is thought of as impersonal, defines the cardinal virtues as 'purity, self-control, detachment, truth and non-violence' and deliberately puts love in an altogether lower category. One finds different scales and priorities of virtues in ages and societies which have different religious starting-points, and it is clear enough that the move away from the now less generally held beliefs of christendom has left morality in some disarray and uncertainty in the West.

It is impossible not to make a connection between belief and ethical conduct. People have occasionally argued that morality is really only a set of rules designed *by society* for its own preservation, which is psychologically bred into children from birth with the necessary guilt reflexes and all. Some plausibility can be made out for such a case, in that without some sort of laws protecting life, property, family relationships and honest dealing, no society could survive. But such a merely utilitarian view of morality does not explain the blossoming of the great virtues that are practised at cost to oneself, even to the very sacrifice of life; it does not give a sufficiently profound explanation of shame, blushing, guilt and conscience, and it does not tally with the account of their motives given by those called to account for a display of noble conduct that brought them into conflict with society.

No, morals, behaviour and activity are ultimately dictated not just by expediency, fear, the need to protect society or self-interest, but by basic belief.

Then what about Christian behaviour? Is there any such thing, and if so, how it is to be defined?

Did Jesus say anything original or distinctive in the matter of conduct, or cannot all his practical teaching be paralleled in Jewish literature? Is his moral teaching essentially private and individual, or is it social, maybe political? Can it be codified and read off from the manual, or is it essentially situation ethics, in which the one principle of love has to be applied without reference to the rule-book, in a particular way relevant to each different situation? Did Jesus point to any absolutes in morality or is an absolute automatically an abstraction, which might then in its turn imply that God himself is subject to some higher law which it represents?

The answer to these questions is that Christian behaviour derives from one absolute only, and that is the character of God himself. There is no law higher than he, but he is utterly self-consistent and so constantly and unchangingly wills what is good. This means that if we want to get some idea of what it is to live and act as a Christian, we have, once again, to go back to where we started, that is, to the character and wishes and emphases of God, as displayed by Jesus himself. It also means that it will not always be possible to state simply and without argument what is the Christian line on matters which Jesus never spoke about or which had not arisen in his time.

In this sort of case, the first rule is to make sure you understand what the issue actually is, what are the facts, palatable and unpalatable, and what are the considerations put by any who might be thought to be technical experts in the subject. Then you take account of any teaching of Jesus that may bear on the subject, and you try to put that in the context of the whole impact of his character — and it is in trying to get this right, of course, that differences will arise among Christians about ethical issues. It is generally useful, on the way to attempting the definition of a Christian position, to rough out a provisional solution, to be tested by trial and error, to see if some factors come to light that you have not previously taken account of. And it always needs to be born in mind that Christian ethical decisions can never be applied, as it were, in a vacuum from scratch: So that for example, if a polygamous animist is converted to Christ, he will have a different problem trying to implement Christ's teaching on marriage from a single westerner who is similarly converted. The situation you are in will undoubtedly affect where you can begin in carrying out what you take to be Christ's command.

But eventually Christian morality is the attempt, from where you actually are, to respond to the nature of God as Christ has shown it, and to reflect that character in your actions, so that your behaviour begins to say Jesus.

Yet in order to understand rightly the Jesus who is God's mirror for us four things need to be born in mind.

1. Some things about God Jesus already took for granted. They may not be stressed, but if we leave out Jesus' Old Testament origins, we shall get a lop-sided picture of him.

2. Jesus was certainly not a law-giver, and whenever the attempt has been made to reduce Jesus' pronouncements into a law, the essential spirit of him is lost. To get hold of the moral emphasis of the man, we must partly listen to his actual sayings and partly stand back and try to catch the general impact he made, thus putting his statements into the framework of his whole personal dynamic.

3. Jesus was not a perennial philosopher or a wandering moralist, but the leader of a religious movement in public. The aims of that movement, some of its basic assumptions and the means he was willing to use to forward its ends will form the material for understanding something of what might be called public Christian morality.

4. By his death and resurrection among men, Jesus made clear some things about the nature of God which were not self-evident before, and we must take account of them in looking at how Christians reflect God's nature.

It is impossible in one lecture to hope to set out a complete compendium of Christian conduct, and my suspicion is that the longer and more detailed such an exposition got, the greater would be the danger of losing Jesus himself in the process. I shall try, therefore, under these four heads and with some illustrations, to see if I can catch the essential flavour and direction of the kind of behaviour and activity that does indeed reflect the character and will of God the Father and our Lord Jesus Christ.

Under my first heading then, there are two things about the nature of God that Jesus seems to have taken for granted. He takes for granted, as I have already argued in the second lecture, that God is the creator of the natural order, standing in the relation of Father to all that is made. When this is considered in relation to moral activity, one has to admit that it is in this area of reference to God as creator that the Christian church has been weakest.

To say, for example, that God is the creator of the world of nature ought to imply that Christians will have a particular care for the way the earth is used. The Old Testament did include a number of kindly laws about letting the earth rest in the seventh year, about not muzzling the ox as it treads out the corn, about hygiene and so on, all inextricably mixed up with other laws which we should more readily think of as moral. Christians, however, particularly since the scientific controversies of the nineteenth century and also since Christianity has come to be urban-based rather than rural-based in its thinking, have tended to abdicate their responsibilities for developing Christian moral criteria, and to leave such matters to scientists or to those who looked chiefly for financial profitability. It is a measure of our failure to take this area of concern seriously that we have trained so few theologians able to speak convincingly to scientists and economists just when so many of them would find such a dialogue helpful; and we should find it hard to know where to look to fill university chairs in such a branch of theology; again, it is small credit to us that Christians can claim little responsibility for the emerging science of ecology, which undoubtedly does raise questions about the morality of the use of the earth and its resources. I recall a Professor of Agriculture who said that the future prosperity of mankind is not a sufficient criterion for assessing our responsibility to the natural environment; we must get back to the Biblical statement, 'the Earth is the Lord's, and the fullness thereof, the round world and they that dwell therein'. We are still a long way from knowing what to make of that.

Both Jesus' parables and his miracles suggest that he took it for granted that human moral activity has to be worked out in the context of a proper relation to the *natural environment*. Again, it would be good if Christians, who claim that God saw all his natural creation to be good, had a better record in regard to the way it has thought about the body, about sex, about human physical achievement. We can probably rightly claim that compassion for the sick has led us to give every encouragement to the development of medical science, and perhaps there have been more contacts between theologians and doctors than with any other scientists. We can probably rightly claim the Christian emphasis on family morality has given women a nobler concept of themselves and has procured for them a greater respect than they previously enjoyed — though a patronising attitude from men is probably not what they are looking for at the present time. But in the whole realm of the relations between men and women, it would be hard to claim that the loudest thing Christians have said over the centuries is 'How good and glorious is our sexual differentiation and all the enlargement of spirit it brings with it'. Now anyone knows that our passions easily outrun our reason; anyone knows that lust is an ugly thing; anyone knows that the exploitation of sex for money is one of the nastiest features of today's commercial entertainment world; and anyone with any sense of responsibility will want to protest, will want to offer guidelines for not falling into many of the traps, will often recommend curbs on passion. But it is a pity that Christians have again and again been heard first saying that sex is dangerous and doubtful even a devilish thing, rather than *first* a marvellous thing, one of God's greatest gifts for our loving and our delighting in one another, which *therefore* requires that we handle it with reverence. It would take a bit of managing but it would be a good thing if Church dances were the most hilariously imaginative and happiest of all dances — and I know places where they are — and if Christian families were the most rumbustiously enjoyable and natural environments for young people to discover how lovely and fascinating members of the other sex are. When you get your degree, you get a hood. It is a sobering thought that the holy monks of the middle ages pulled those hoods down over their eyes as they walked along for fear of being tempted by the sight of a woman. Jesus has some tough things to say about how men should look at women, but he himself, who never married but presumably knew what it is to be a man as we are, mixed easily in all sorts of company, enjoyed our differences and seems to have brought out the best in even the worst of his Father's children.

Jesus took it for granted that God was creator. We have still some way to go before we have worked out the main-lines of a Christian morality in the area of God's creation.

Jesus also took it for granted that God was the source and definer of what we ordinarily think of as moral conduct.

This sounds so evident as to be hardly worth mentioning, but it is in fact of some considerable significance. There are religions which have no particular connection with morality at all. The Greek gods, for example, were hardly models of moral probity, and the Greek ideas of the good were worked out independently of them. It is not far from the truth to say that in Hinduism morality and spirituality are two distinct departments of religion: you need to pass in morality before you can go on and graduate in spirituality, which is concerned with something quite different from moral conduct.

Again, some religions which major on spiritual experience see bodily life as hostile to the spirit, so that they either require a repressive morality in order to concentrate wholly on the spirit, or else they can say that the body is so unimportant that nothing you do in the body can have any effect one way or the other on the spirit.

But the Jews, who first knew God as their Deliverer from Egypt, learnt in the Law revealed on Mount Sinai the nature and character and will of him who had chosen them, and from then onwards their deepest spirituality had an unfailing moral element to it, which Jesus rightly captured in his summary of the two loves. And as one reads the history of Israel and sees how hard the Jews found it to get anywhere near to keeping God's law, it remains an astonishing wonder how the prophets knew with such certainty that God could not tolerate immorality and idolatry, how they were able to set out moral demands both in the personal and social fields, so sure they could claim God's very word for them. The Ten

Commandments, considered as a revelation of the way God is and wants it, make a striking document, with its duty to God and to man bound inextricably together, with its unusual command to rest one day in seven and so also to take holidays as part of the way a man remains alert to God and truly human in himself, with its scrutiny even of motive in the last command about covetousness. And it is further worth remarking that the Law was given in the context of what was regarded as that great *mystic* encounter — when Moses went up into the thick darkness — where God was.

God the creator of all things and the creator of them good, God who revealed his holy and righteous nature in Law, that was the God whom Jesus knew as his Father. Anything he said himself was against that background.

So under my second heading, is it possible to get a grasp of the main moral emphasis of Jesus' own teaching? A difficult business; easier, I think, to try to describe the impact of his person in terms of what seem to have been his priorities.

The first striking thing is that there is no aspect of the life and activity of Jesus which is not at one and the same time an aspect of his communion with his Father. It is impossible to make a division between the spiritual and the ethical life of Jesus — they are one seamless robe. He summed up the law in the two commandments to love God and neighbour and saw them as inseparable, and in his ministry everything he did for his neighbours is an expression of his awareness of the immediacy of God. So if we follow Jesus, and are asked, 'What is Christian ethics', it is first of all prayer, it is first of all and in everything having to do with God. The great saints of the spirit have not been dreamers nor escapists, but again and again men and women of immense practical competence, but wherever they came they brought with them a sense that there were resources of goodness and hope beyond those that men can provide by their own intelligence, because they lived in prayer, gave time to prayer and worked with a discipline that allowed them time to pray. We look around at the world with its rising tide of desperate and heartbreaking problems and feel there can be no time for anything but ceaseless *activity*. Luther said, 'I have so much to do that I cannot get on without three hours a day of praying'. Undoubtedly the world will look different if we are rooted in prayer, and we shall bring better help if we have allowed proper space for God in all our living and thinking. Christian morality is first praying, and that will involve all the practical things like alarm-clocks, rules for rising and budgetting time for God, setting oneself to read in order to get beyond the elementary stage, learning how to listen to God's word, developing the capacity to respond to the Holy Spirit's guidance and letting him be turning one's whole heart and will towards God. It is this loving of God that turns the loving of neighbour from being a sterile legalism into just, true and heartfelt service.

The second feature of the ethical impact of Jesus is the utterly uncompromising, profound simplicity of it all. His contemporaries accepted God's law as holy and assumed, as any one might, that laws apply to particular cases, and so they set limits to what was permissible, examined the propriety of individual acts, and developed a thoroughly practical but somewhat limiting casuistry. Jesus cuts through all this. He assumes that the prescription, 'Thou shalt not kill' is not just a prohibition applying to some extreme situation, with a further consideration of extenuating circumstances. All this is brushed aside. If you sneer at a person as someone not worth bothering with, if you write someone off as contemptible, you have simply failed to see what the commandment is about; and you aren't, on the positive side, just to act lovingly to those you already get on with — plenty of people without faith can manage that — you are to have the loving disposition in all circumstances and to all, without frontiers and without limit, just as God does. And there is no suggestion that if you can't manage 100% of this attitude, sixty per cent will get you a pass — rather, if your eye or your hand or your foot get in the way of this total holiness, get rid of them. And whether it is murder, adultery or lying, in Jesus' eyes God's law is not about those actions which are forbidden, it is about the complete response to God's own character in a heart that loves all the time, in a heart that is pure enough to look freely and openly at anyone, in a heart that has no other desire than to speak the plain truth to whoever it be. It needs to be said that those people who claim that the essence of Christianity is in the Sermon on the Mount and that is all we need, not a lot of theology, need to be taken at their word. If one takes Jesus seriously, Christian morality asks for nothing less than the total conversion of the heart, and the moral demands of Christ will drive a man, as the spiritual understanding of the law drove St. Paul, to realise that he may be able to do the right deeds, or at any rate refrain from the wrong ones, but is quite incapable of discovering within himself the wholesome heart, and can only get anywhere near the sort of morality Jesus asked for in broken dependence on a Saviour.

Now you might think that a person who set forth and practised this quite uncompromising morality would have been a tense, rather forbidding, censorious person. And there's the paradox. No-one ever gave the impression of a greater freedom. Christ's morality is somehow a liberating morality. He offended some of his contemporaries because he appeared to play fast and loose with rules and conventions, healed on the sabbath and was happy to eat in the company of people the religious leaders either disapproved of or felt they would be corrupted by. But this is not because Jesus is some sort of liberal who says the rules don't matter, but because he lives them out at such depth that they have ceased to be rules. We call him Saviour because he sets men free. He was most marvellously free in himself, and all Christian morality is meant to free, to enlarge, to release, by deepening and anchoring people so that there is no conflict at the bottom of them, but that, like him, they are wholeheartedly given in one direction.

The other obvious element in the impact Jesus made, it might be simplest to call love, if his own attitudes are allowed to define the word, for, as far as I can see, Jesus did not talk as much about love as some of his followers have done. However, in relation to those he came across casually, if that's a proper way of speaking, Jesus gave them one and all his total attention. He responded to their words, their requests, their witticisms, and evidently warmed to some of their personalities quite naturally. But one after another had his complete attention to such an extent that before him they felt in the presence of ultimate judgement or salvation; in his presence they saw the essential truth about themselves, and while with some, his gaze or maybe his prescription was fierce, his attention invariably offered hope, healing, a summons to a way forward into newness. In relation to those who followed him as disciples, love meant that he expected them to work together, he rebuked and praised them in public in front of one another, with no private talks in his study; he shocked them, tested them, entrusted his ministry to them and shamed their quarrels. He gave them no opportunity of pronouncing on one another's fitness for his service but gave them to one another as brethren and above all, gave ministry to them without reserve to make that brotherhood reality. To all men, including those who opposed him, Jesus showed himself so completely identified in love that he could not but die for them as he had lived with them.

I have attempted to get the flavour of the moral impact Jesus had, and suggested that it arises from a marvellous mixture of prayer, uncompromisingness, freedom and love. To be practical Christians, to be the Church of Christ in its conduct and behaviour, is to get the mix right — and it is very difficult to get it right. Sometimes we have tried to separate practical ethics from spirituality, dividing ascetic or mystical and moral theology, whereas Jesus makes no such division. Sometimes we have tried to follow him in being uncompromising, but have succeeded only in being legalistic rather than setting men free.

Sometimes we have waved the word 'love' over every situation without remembering the passionate fierceness of Jesus' Old Testament forebears who loved well because they also hated well, and without paying attention to the content Jesus put into personal relationships. How, for example, are we to express the real flavour of Jesus when we are asked for practical help in regard to the remarriage of people who have been divorced? In his actual teaching, Jesus is far stricter than his contemporaries, declaring quite simply that marriage after divorce is adultery, but when he was faced with an actual woman taken in adultery, he treated her with a gracefulness that convicted the consciences of her accusers and made a new person of her, and maybe, once again, it is the undivided conviction at the heart of his teaching that enables the freedom of action in face of the individual. But then Jesus is not legislating. How are we to translate what he said into some sort of *code of practice* which will at the *same time* allow us to offer hope to those in need? Clearly this is too large a subject to argue here, but I think we have to try to remain both *strict* and *loving*, not resting content to turn strictness into a law and hard luck on those who have failed, not offering a love which has no obvious root in strong saving conviction.

There is one further point to be made about the attempt to live out the practical example of Jesus. The sort of moral teaching Jesus gave in the Sermon on the Mount calls for absolute perfection: we are to reflect the Father's character and nothing else, both in outward action and in the very springs of our instincts. Now the experience of the greatest saints—and this is what sets Jesus, our only example, apart from us—is that the closer they drew in love to their Lord, the more they were aware of repeated failures and of the depths of inward unconvertedness. It is, I think, bad theology to speak of human beings as totally depraved, if by that is meant that we have become completely evil with no good impulses left, for this would be neither true to experience, nor would it allow that we were in any sense sustained by God who created us in love. But it is true that there is no action that we can ever take, however deeply spiritual, which we do not find stained, spoiled, distorted, misdirected in some way or other by the sin that has got into the very springs of us. This means that a Christian moral position, aiming to follow Christ's command of perfection, has to begin with the admission of failure and utter imperfection. Now we are often ready enough to admit this in formal prayers, but find it harder to accept it when others tell us so, and are frequently censorious of others just in those areas where it would be more fitting if we accepted that we are weak ourselves. To be perfect as a Christian starts with our having no illusions at all about ourselves, and this ought to put a particular flavour into our judgement of others. It is hardly possible, nor is it right, to avoid making comments and maybe fierce judgements upon actions or proposed courses of action, but they come better from those who sound as if they were aware of living with temptation themselves, and were identified with the condition of all men. But has not Christ saved us from sin, and do we not censure vice in others out of concern for his honour? Of course, to know Christ is to feel the awfulness of wickedness more sharply; of course to know his saving grace means that morality ceases to be slavish duty and becomes our loving response to the nature of him who saved us, but we continue to call him Saviour just because we go on and on discovering the onion-like layers of sinfulness in ourselves that need his gracious work, and must surely know that we are in no position to speak to others as if we stood secure in some achieved righteousness of our own. We have to sound like Jesus in our moral pronouncements, and it is the tone of his voice, not our own, that we have to reproduce by humble loving dependence on him.

The other strands in Christ's moral attitude — freedom and love ought to appear in the way the Church behaves. While upholding a morality of perfection, it ought also to be a body where people find they are really made free; while not afraid of the grind of duty, it ought to set men free from the mentality of legalism; while strong in defence of a positive orthodoxy, it ought not to be led into witch-hunts nor to stifle the free spirit with the tyranny of the current consensus or trend; and in all things, it ought to wean people away from self-justification into a more and more instinctive expectation of mutual forgiveness. And love should mean that Christians should be learning among themselves always to listen to others, never to sneer, caricature, misunderstand or misrepresent, but to affirm them to the point where we all can face truth bravely and find our capacities maximised and enlarged with spiritual grace.

My third heading requires that we ask how do we reflect in our practical activity the character and impact of Christ, the leader of a movement?

Let us be clear at the outset: Jesus was not a political leader, and in the one plainly political question put to him in regard to the payment of taxes to an occupying power, his reply must have been disappointingly tame to political radicals and nationalist revolutionaries. There is certainly no political philosophy that can be based directly on his teaching, though undoubtedly there are political philosophies which can never be made to square with it. But Jesus was ultimately crucified on a political charge by the secular governor of the country, who whatever he thought of the motives of the religious leaders who brought Jesus before him, knew that enough colour could be given to the charge for it to be impossible for him simply to dismiss it. So what is distinctive about Jesus' public activity, and is there a Christian style in the way we attempt to follow him in our world and our problems?

Four distinct features mark Jesus out in the way he led his movement.

First, it was always and all the time a spiritual movement. *God* is *king*; how can all human activity come to accept, understand and reflect that truth? Now that question is an individual question, a social question and a political question, and it is going to involve what must be called political activity, because God had already started the process by calling Israel among the nations, and Jesus came to fulfil that process. But we are talking about a spiritual process, and Jesus never lost sight of that end.

Secondly, Jesus was a poor man, of doubtful parentage, a layman, a non-establishment man. In no way did he stress this, but it meant that the disadvantaged at once recognised him as someone who understood them and spoke for them, and authorities and those with vested interests tended to feel threatened by him. For centuries now, Jesus' teaching has been set out by those who *are* establishment men, and this automatically gives it a different flavour and tendency. The New Testament texts about submitting to authority sound different when they are insisted upon by those who are in authority and have a personal stake in the maintenance of the status quo, rather than when they come from those who are talking to their fellows groaning under the same insolence of office. We cannot, of course, speak or act from any other position than the one we actually occupy, but Jesus' own position ought to be deeply impressed on the consciences of all Christian authority figures, to make them not only wisely responsible but always and automatically sensitive to the underdog, and that includes the noisy, rude and illogical underdog. It would perhaps be salutary if every Christian leader carried with him in his wallet a letter of resignation, to be dated and sent in if ever he found his position made it no longer possible for him to act as a champion of those without rights. Jesus is called Saviour, because as a liberator he stood naturally among those whose freedom was limited by their circumstances.

Thirdly, Jesus was a superb leader, a superb practical activist. This involves a clear definition of his ultimate goal, which was to persuade all Israel, right up to the High Priests who had the constituted authority to commit Israel to the decision, that he was the one sent by God to gather it into the fulfilment of God's destiny for it.

It involves intelligent envisaging of long-term strategy and short-term tactic, a checking along the way to be sure that the way things were going still served the ultimate goal. So Jesus laid a strong base in Galilee where the situation was favourable, before pressing his claim on the capital; in the feeding of the 5,000 we see that he had roused Galilee to quite a fever pitch of expectation, but was bold enough to dismiss the crowd when they wanted to make him king because he saw that their ends were not yet his — just as Gandhi called off the salt marches for exactly the same reasons. He had to take special measures in the last week in the capital, because he was already aware of the defection of Judas.

It involves an eye to timing, so that actions will have the desired effect rather that go off as damp squibs. Although he foresaw his death, he did not intend to allow himself simply to be bumped off in any backstreets, but to be condemned, if he was, on the charge of claiming to be God's Messiah for Israel by the one person who had the right to decide for Israel whether he was or not, and in the trial he was careful not to get bogged down in arguing over irrelevancies, so that the High Priest should be forced to ask that particular question. Jesus conducted his public ministry with masterly intelligence, and Christians in their public activity should not suppose that mere good-natured opportunism is a sufficient substitute for the theologically directed intelligent activity.

But fourthly, at the climax of his public activity, having brought Israel to face the all-important question of its destiny, he accepted the right of the authorities to condemn and execute him. He did not organise force to overthrow them; he did not call upon supernatural or divine powers to worst them; he did not separate from them and try and set up his kingdom elsewhere. Every one of these alternatives, which have come to tempt those who in any way have tried to follow him in public activity, would have involved separating himself from God's Israel and regarding at least some in Israel as his enemies. He accepted the cross because it means complete identification to the very end with the Yeses and the Noes and all the host of Don't knows, and because it means that God is still to be utterly trusted when things look their worst, just as he is when they seem to be going well, trusted in the conviction that out of human *obedience* God can bring a more perfect good than even human ingenuity at its best. The cross is the uniquely distinctive mark of all Christian public activity, and it is the hardest of all to bear. It is hard to get the timing of it right, for the cross is not just having the temperament of a doormat; it is hard to recognise God's cross held out to us in the appalling choices that arise out of the antecedent activity; it is hard to bear the cross trustfully and willingly; yet without the trustful, loving heart, it loses its virtue. The cross is the final badge in all Christian activity, but because it is such an astonishing and incredible badge, we find few who realise it is meant to be worn, few who have practised for it, few who lecture about its application in lectures on Christian Social Ethics, few who have borne it in the sort of situations that really call for it. There are lots of minor situations, in matters of personal relations, between husbands and wives, in the conduct of Church meetings, where we ought to be practising for the cross, but if we even catch a glimpse of its awful shape, as a rule we hastily say, 'Oh no, this is not a situation where that way of thinking applies — I am standing for a principle and must stick to it come what may by whatever means'; and so we have hardly the experience to consider the application of the cross to larger issues of Christian obedience.

Jesus, the Messiah, kept a spiritual goal before him; he was truly placed to be recognised as a liberator; he was a bold activist and a very intelligent planner, and at the bottom of all his instincts there was a cross branded into his soul. And once again it will be clear that such a style can only grow out of a life that is lived by prayer all through.

When you think of the application of Jesus' example in this sphere to present-day problems, it is worth while recalling that perhaps the classic discussion of the cross in the New Testament arises from a consideration of the relation of slaves and masters, or as we should say, of industrial relations. Now we live today under democratic freedoms the slaves never knew, there are traditional rights that have been won and that no one would think of going back on, whereas slaves had no rights at all; the social situation in England is not such that confrontation is a sine qua non of industrial discussion, whereas equal relations between even well-disposed masters and slaves are unthinkable, and there is a wealth of industrial labour relations experience, so that our situation is very different from that of the slaves of the First Epistle of Saint Peter, but it is a pity that we haven't done a bit more on the application of Christ's own public attitude, to industrial bargaining, since presumably the two key points in I Peter, that Christ's is the only model for Christians to follow and that it is redemptive in its effect, hold true.

How is the public Jesus to be followed in situations, say in Northern Ireland or South Africa, that seem to cry out for immediate, and if necessary violent reform? We begin by remembering that he was one of those against whom legal violence was employed—so he knows the boiling provocation of it, especially in the face of injustice.

Now violence is either the passionate, unpremeditated reaction to the office-holders with all the police at their back. Or it is the calculated theory that force will gain concessions that nothing else will.

But Jesus trusts that in God there is a justice never defeated which will ultimately be brought down to earth; and he stands for the liberty not only of the oppressed, but also of the oppressor. So as *the* way to the revealing of God's justice, he is prepared to bear violence without bitterness himself but not to inflict it on others. And there is no other way for Christians.

And that leads naturally to that terrible area of violence — war and all the questions of nuclear armaments.

There are, as everyone knows, many more background considerations relating to nuclear power as a whole, than I can take account of in a few brief words tonight. And of course, this is one of the issues where it makes a difference to the way you speak whether you are in a position to exercise responsibility or not.

As far as the *general principle* is concerned, the case for the immediate abandonment of all production and distribution of nuclear weapons is unanswerable. War is a wicked way of settling disputes in spite of any heroism it may involve; nuclear war is prepared to contemplate unimaginable destruction of life and civilisation, is prepared to pollute the future for whatever generations may survive, and requires the spending of vast millions on unproductive weapons when the larger part of the world's population is under-fed, badly housed, under-educated and without the basic amenities of life.

Again, to argue that nuclear weapons contribute to the defence of these islands is ludicrous nonsense. In any nuclear war between the super powers, anything like England will be simply obliterated. Now it is not difficult for you and me to arrive at these conclusions. But if you are a politician in power, if you are a Christian politician in power, it is a far harder thing knowing how to set about implementing them.

A government, for instance, has to act on the basis of informed popular consent. How easy would it be to be sure there was an informed mandate for immediate nuclear disarmament? A government, again, must be concerned for the defence of the country. But the defence of this country is not an independent matter — it is wrapped-up with a number of arrangements with other friendly countries. It is not an easy decision to know whether and how to disentangle ourselves from these alliances — or even to dientangle ourselves from the nuclear ingredient in these alliances. But more important, as it seems to me, although the Salt Treaty and the Security Conference produce so painfully few results, they do bring all the nations involved into negotiations, and thereby some inching forward in the way of personal trust, some little bridgeheads into International understanding are — however fragilely — being formed. And since the true solution to all our war problems comes not from being able to establish unchallengeable positions of strength, not from hopefully setting quixotic examples of defencelessness, but from working towards International organs of control, where International Police will eventually replace National Armies, it seems to me that it would be deeply irresponsible to withdraw from that exasperatingly slow business of International negotiation and relationship, which are the only way of laying the foundation ultimately for a more International government.

So to me, just as any Christian, it seems that there is first a very good case for building up a stronger and stronger anti-nuclear lobby of intelligent, young, responsible people all over the world, so that politicians get the feel of who it is they are representing; secondly that defence ministers and others in that field should be preparing step by step smaller-scale bargaining-counters, so that a continual movement towards nuclear disarmament can be brought about in an atmosphere of International trust rather than to be felt to be either stone-walling or else a con-trick in which one side is simply getting the better of the other; and thirdly that there should be a real praying for political leaders who have to make decisions on timing—when a gesture will be understood as a positive contribution, and when it will be seen to be provocative or simply useless.

Christians have *both* to support politicians by strong moral conviction; and also to recognise that it is in their and everyone's interest that politicians should be as good, experienced, brave, tireless, idealistic — but as professional politicians as possible.

Friends, to follow the public Jesus is a very difficult business, and we do well not to outlaw one another but to help one another by love and argument, as we fumble our way forward to actions that are meant truly to reflect him.

My last heading — an attempt to see Christian activity as a reflection of God's nature — suggested that there are some things about the nature of God that become clear as the later result of pondering on the implications of Jesus' incarnation. I have already spoken of the Holy Spirit as one who works the character and the powers of Jesus himself into the Church and into the individual, and I want, perhaps provocatively, to emphasize that order. As I read the New Testament, Christians are made holy, not primarily as individuals working through devotional tasks of self-examination, but primarily through their relations with one another. The fruits of the spirit are corporate virtues — virtues that grow from bearing, loving, understanding, challenging, forgiving, loyally backing one another up; and not just the virtues of the individual stiff upper lip — a virtue for which I have no scorn.

However, the experience of the Holy Spirit led Christian thinkers to realize that the nature of God was less simple than at first they might have imagined. Already the first monotheistic Jewish Christians had been driven to accepting that Jesus must be reckoned divine and also that part of the truth about him was his relationship with his father. When, after Pentecost and the end of the physical appearance of Jesus, Christians began to realize that the instrument by which they were inwardly experiencing the continuing nearness of Jesus was no less than a divine presence in them, they came to see that God had been threefold in his activity towards them and this implied, not just three alternative modes of action, but three modes of being, in that one and the same God. The church was led into accepting that God is Trinity in his essential nature.

Obviously we are competent to speak only of our experience of God's threefold activity, while recognizing that it is nevertheless the activity of one and the same God. Here Dorothy Sayers' analogy of the activity of an author writing a book is a helpful one. The book is first the conception in the mind of the author; secondly, it is the uttered, typed, printed, bound visible work that you can buy on Paragon Station; but then it is also the digestion of that book by the reader until he has made the original thought of the author his own. This is a useful illustration to show that if God is to reveal himself to us and in us in the way Jesus suggests he does, revelation is essentially a threefold activity. This does not tell us anything about the inner Trinitarian life of God himself, except that if true divinity is met with in the originating Father, in the historical Jesus and in the inner experience of the Spirit, then we must suppose that these are, in the technical language of theology, three persons in the one God, about whose relationship some rudimentary things at least can be posited.

If it is this God Christian action seeks to represent, then there are some fascinating implications.

In all our human experience, we find ourselves in tension between the individual and the corporate, the one and the many. Our experience of love, for instance, makes us long to be completely one with the beloved, and yet love itself implies a relationship and not an absorption. Psychologists minister on the one hand to those who can't make any relationship with others, and on the other to those who live in fear of being swallowed up and their personality sucked out by a demanding or over-possessive companion. Religion itself lives in uneasy tension between those who give ultimate authority to the individual conscience and those who give it to the Church, and suffers on the extremes from intractable individualists and boringly orthodox gramophones. The trinitarian nature of God holds out to us the hope that as we grow nearer and nearer to him, both our individuality is affirmed as of eternal worth, and also the possibility of ultimate oneness and the recovery of the whole creation's unity in him.

I suppose this lecture would have been a good deal shorter if I had simply said that Christian activity is plain straighforward obedience to the double command to love God and neighbour. Anyone who thinks it is straightforward probably hasn't tried very hard. What I have tried to do here is to argue that the only way we can effectively love our extraordinary range of neighbours is by translating into action our loving response to the actual God Jesus has shown him to be.

There are religions which are in essence perennial philosophies. They define what is good regardless of time and change, paint the picture of the good man, the good life, the good society, insisting that these good things are independent of historical circumstance, are appropriate to any age or place, and are not modified by past or future. There are religions which are essentially cyclic, which speak of the circling years bringing round the age of gold, that declare that history repeats itself, that expansion follows contraction, wave succeeds trough unceasingly, that human existence is but a shaking of the kaleidoscope, a mere altering of the details of the unchanging pattern with no thread of purpose running through the process that can possibly be identified. There are religions which assign all our weariness and maladies to change and chance, and to the fluctuations of history, and which see the true goal of life as the settling of oneself in that ultimate detachment from the wheel of change, into the changeless consciousness of pure spirit.

To all such religions, history is of no ultimate significance. I recall an Indian philosopher saying, 'What can particular events in history tell us of timeless truth?'

On the other hand, perhaps more in the West where our culture has been affected by aspects of Christianity, there has sometimes been a feverish concern with movement and change, as we feel ourselves at some times hounded and driven forward farther than we want to go, or at others eagerly stretching out our hands to goals we think within our grasp. That great nineteenth century will-o'-the-wisp, progress, undoubtedly was a spur to the achieving of a number of proximate goals even if long-term utopias eluded it. Today's words are growth and development, that go with the feeling that if you are not developing you must be stagnating, if you are not growing you must be dying, that change is more real than stability, that if a thing has been discovered to be scientifically possible, then it must be put into practice regardless of the consequences.

Whichever way it is with us, whichever tradition of thought we have grown up with or been most affected by, it is a fact that this sense of time's winged chariot hurrying near us — as certain also of our own poets have said — of ourselves being carried along by forces of history which jostle us out of contentment and allow us no possibility of saying, 'Stop the world, I want to get off', granting us no place of settled peace, is an element in all human experience, and perhaps at no time so strongly as at the present. It is an element all religious systems have to come to grips with, it is an element which they invest with particular significance, but because change and movement exercise such remorseless pressure on all men, the popular versions of these religions sometimes tend to obscure what they really have to say.

As far as Christianity is concerned, the central paradox is that in Jesus Christ, the Eternal God engaged himself in time, the Changeless God suffered himself to be buffeted about by the changes and chances of this fleeting world. Now Jesus' own prayer, Thy kingdom *come*, at once confirms the Old Testament sense that human history is neither aimless nor meaningless, but is set a direction and a goal, through all its vicissitudes, by God himself; and this perhaps sharpens the significance and the pain of those elements of human experience where man's mortality, his sense of destiny and of accountability are all brought into focus. Yet along with this emphasising of the onward sweep of history, God is also revealed in Christ as the God who gives meaning, who sets contentment in the heart, who ensures stability, who provides the necessary element of reliability and so of hopefulness beyond all the frenetic weariness of change. We might say that in Christ, changeless eternity is seen to have a firm grip on time and transience, imparting to all human experience both immediacy and direction, and asking for faith while ensuring ultimate certainty. It is this flavour of Christianity that I want to explore further in this lecture. But before developing the sense of richness this Christian perspective is intended to give to human living, let us first look at those notes in human experience that remind man that this life alone cannot tell him his whole story; let us stop for a moment over what are often called the Last Things.

First, death.

The death of man is not like the death of the rest of the animal creation. As far as we can tell, when their time has come, they curl up and are gone, with no compelling evidence that the event was horrifying, with no funeral ceremonies, with no dwelling on bereavement. But for man, death is always an affront, an anxiety, a horror, something to be defied — or else, something to be perceived with new eyes.

To some, death means the agonising thought that the world will carry on satisfactorily enough with its business when I am gone, will perhaps put up a memorial or deliver a funeral oration for me, but will not disintegrate because I am no longer there to put out a steadying hand. Have I left nothing behind, has all my intensity of living and feeling no ultimate significance?

To others, our longer lives of today have only prolonged the frighteningness of death itself: as powers of body, of mind, of feeling weaken and fade, as friends and contemporaries die or become inaccessible, increasing loneliness and diminishing horizons put a question-mark over any meaning to life at all, and give some colour to the Exit-men in their search for a way of escape.

To others, the approach of death means the realisation that I have no more chances. The things I hoped but failed to do will now never be done. My sins can now no longer be amended nor my character reformed; I am fixed in the mediocrity I have achieved. With visions unfulfilled, I am reduced by my failures to a shrunken shadow of the self I hoped to be and set out in my youth to be; and however thankful I am for all the good things life and people have given me, I cannot but be aware of vast areas of myself never brought into play, vast possibilities of experience never explored, vast tracts of time utterly wasted, wrong paths pursued, vain or damaging relationships entered into, so many things done that ought never to have been done, and so many more left undone that my conscience tells me I had the opportunity of doing and ought to have done.

To others, all this means that death is fearful because it means judgement. In the hour of death when all pretences are stripped away and excuses seen to be hollow, when I stand shrivelled and naked, I cannot but recognise that I shall not pass scrutiny by my own standard, by other men's standard and certainly not by God's. And judgement leads on to the fear of what death opens on to. Is it retribution, is it cold nothingness, is it some unimaginable, maybe intolerable, prolongation of consciousness, does it make any provision for the achievements and loves of this life to bear any immortal fruit, and if so, does that mean that the shames of this life will pursue me for ever? Is it just a horrid precipice over which I am to be pushed, falling for ever into oblivion?

Can any sense at all be made of all man's greatness and glory here if, after seventy or eighty years he is thrown away, reverts to dust and is forgotten? If death ends it all, and if one rejects as brave but self-deceptive the humanist shaking of the fist in the face of Nothingness, can there be any incentive for living other than a totally selfish life? Death, the great Enemy that all men without exception must come to, death, the great question-mark over all man's striving — what can be said in the face of death?

There is only one reliable piece of evidence about death and its significance, only one man who has returned from death and told us a different story, only one hope held out of turning this inexorable fate into the gateway to unlimited life. But what that Man points to needs presently to be put into its proper context.

The second reminder to man of his finitude we have already touched on — the sense that he lives under judgement, must one day be caught up with, have to render up his accounts and hear the true verdict pronounced upon him. Perhaps this fear has always been a diffused one, at some times, for some people, sharpened to a fierce anguish, at present, for many, and to our loss, I suspect, somewhat blunted. At all times, judgement seems to have been a blundering haphazard business, nothing like as just as we should have thought it ought to be.

For the conviction that there is a judgement for each individual and for mankind as a whole, fearful though it may be, is nevertheless a mark of hope, a token of the faith that we do not live in a meaningless world, but in a world moral to its core, a world in which the wicked will not always get away with it nor the good fail of their just praise, a world in which our law-processes are but a fallible reflection of an eternal pattern of justice, a world in which somewhere, somehow, some time, right will have been shown to be right and wrong to be wrong. Christian faith has tended to speak of judgement in three ways, to attach it to three moments, that cannot easily be put together but that represents each of them a truth.

It is the work of the Holy Spirit to bring you face to face with Jesus Christ *now*, where you are shown the essential truth about yourself *now* and offered the ultimate choice before you *now*, just as Jesus said that all the stored up judgement of the past came to rest *now* on the generation that saw him. To meet Jesus and to turn away is to turn away into the night, to be judged.

Then, the moment of *death* has often been felt to be the moment of judgement, the moment when there are no further possibilities of deception and no further excuse, no more hope of self-justification, no more time for putting things off. So death is still properly seen as a great moment of truth and the last chance for repentance, for turning to Christ and for hearing those astonishing words spoken to one in a very evil case, 'Today thou shalt be with me in Paradise'. And it's a fairly robust honesty that says that the notion of a second chance after death doesn't make much sense, though who knows if death might bring a truer recognition of Christ himself than this life has granted to some.

But in addition the Bible speaks of a *Last* Judgement, of a great assize when all shall appear before God and the books be opened and the accounts settled once and for all. This clearly makes sense in that both a man's good and a man's evil bear fruit and produce effects for good and ill that may far outlast his death. We all live helped or crippled by the love and the sins of our parents, long after they are gone; people are converted or led astray by books written centuries ago; and the wrong-headed decisions of political leaders may keep men in misery long after they are dead and gone. It is not foolish to think that there must be a moment when the long process is called to a halt, when all men are seen at their true long-term worth, when the balance sheet of all the effects of the good and evil they have done is finally totted up and a line drawn across the book, and true justice is done to strong and weak, to those with influence and those without, to sane and insane, oppressor and oppressed, to beautiful and deformed, to good and bad alike. A final judgement — a moral world requires it, impossible of conception though it be. The prospect of final true judgement by God, who knows the secrets of every heart, has always been a frightening one — and life is poorer when this is not so — for however good a face we may put on for our neighbours, there is none but the most conceited who does not recognise at some moment or another that 'in thy sight shall no man living be justified'. But once again, Jesus has given new meaning to judgement, so that fear turns out to be only the obverse of hope. Because in his life-time, Jesus was himself one of the great majority who never achieve due recognition or a fair share of the world's goods, and because he was so evidently misjudged, judgement by him brings hope that in the last assize all men will be treated fairly and the voice of the deprived will be heard. Moreover, he made it clear that we are judged finally not simply on our deeds, but on whether our deeds direct us towards or away from himself. And he is not only the truest of all judges because he lived to the full the life of our humanity, but he is at the same time the Saviour in whom we find our ultimate justification and resting place.

But to speak of judgement forces us to speak of that other great traditional end-point — hell. What, if anything, is to be said about hell, once preached with great fervour, to the salvation it is said, of some, to the needless terror, it is said, of others, to the total rejection of Christianity as vengeful, and vindictive, it is said, by others; not preached much these days yet still on the statute-book. Is there anything to be said about hell or are we too modern for that?

It needs to be said as a sober fact that hell is spoken of in the more pictorial parts of the New Testament, the Gospels and Revelation. St. Paul, a more abstract writer, has nothing to say about it at all, apparently seeing nothing but extinction for all those not raised with Christ. And the medieval elaboration that grew up out of the over-literal dwelling upon the frightening sketches in Revelation is not the place to look for any reasoned attempt to state what if anything hell means. For let there be no doubt about it — the whole concept of hell as endless punishment witnessed by those now in eternal bliss presents terrible problems for any Christian theologian. Let us first accept that if the world is to be seen as an expression of God's justice, a place must be reserved for the stark reality of ultimate judgement; let us accept that we must maintain man's God-given freedom to resist God to the last; let us accept that we do, already in this life, see people degenerating and their humanity dissolving away, apparently beyond any possibility of recovery or redemption; let us accept that as far as I myself am concerned, a negative verdict on me and what I have been is a terribly real possibility. But on the other hand, if God has to write off any of his creatures or even more if he has to condemn any to endless torment, it seems that he, the *Almighty*, has been defeated in his purpose; and again, if we admit that he at some point gives up the hope of redeeming any of his creatures, then it seems that his nature of love has finally worn out and changed, unless anyone is prepared to devise an argument for hell that sees it as an expression of God's love. These are formidable objections to any doctrine of hell, and yet simply to ignore it leaves us with an uncomfortably lopsided picture. Perhaps the most useful thing we can say is that the concept of hell represents a necessary paradox that as human beings we must preserve. Hell represents man's ultimate and indefeasible freedom to say No to God, but if God is to remain true to his revealed and changeless nature, we must also maintain that he will never take No for an answer.

To Lady Julian who could not see, in the face of the Church's teaching on Hell, how all could be well and all manner of things could be well, if God saved his word and was faithful to what he had declared in scripture, God said, 'I shall save my word in all things, and I shall make all things well'. Farther than that it is not possible to go.

Death, hell and judgement, those great classical reminders that we live in time and that there is an end that confronts us all. Certainly, Jesus offers the possibility of looking at them all humbly but boldly and seeing them with quite new eyes, but, perhaps surprisingly, the New Testament has not got a great deal to say about any of them, and it has even less to say about their joyful reverse side, the eternal life of heaven, and nothing much to help us to imagine it.

The plain fact of the matter is that the main emphasis of the New Testament is not on these issues. It is not the happy or tragic end of the individual that occupies the forefront of the New Testament concern and that gives it its peculiar dynamic. The New Testament is overwhelmingly concerned with the fulfilment of *God's* great plan for *his kingdom* and that is entirely bound up with the person of Jesus Christ. It is against *that* backdrop, *that* hope for a whole future of glory, that the destiny of any individual comes into focus. What gives the New Testament its special flavour is the sense that with the appearance of Jesus, *human history* has reached its final and decisive climax, and that from then onward there is a racing of the blood to see that decisive intervention made the reality for the whole of human life and the whole of creation.

One of the hardest of all problems for anyone attempting to set forth the Christian faith in its authentic tone is to know what to make of this New Testament flavour and what underlies it.

First there is the job of interpreting the very unmanageable evidence in a balanced way.

Then, one has to ask what the church in history has done with the inheritance the New Testament has handed down, and where, as it seems, that inheritance is puzzling, whether it is in fact binding on the church.

And thirdly, you have to ask what, if anything, it means for Christian living and preaching today.

What is the evidence we are talking about?

Well, first of all, the very appearance of Jesus itself confronts us with paradoxes.

Has he or hasn't he blown a hole in history?

There is his announcement, 'The time is fulfilled', which means that the time of waiting is over, God is no longer holding his hand, history has reached its climactic turning point. No more ordinary history ahead of you; and John the Baptist is described in Elijah terms at the beginning of the gospel to make it absolutely clear that he is the forerunner of the long-awaited *End*. Jesus' coming is a kind of gasp, a sudden focusing of everything into sharpness after centuries of blurred uncertainty. The End upon us. No more time for existence — all eyes on the immediate to come.

Yet on the other hand what actually happened wherever Jesus was, at any rate at the beginning of his ministry, was such an outburst of happiness, such a changing of water into wine, such an experience of presentness, that it seemed in some ways to push all thoughts of any kind of future off the agenda, so that some have interpreted the enigmatic words, 'The kingdom of God has come near' to mean, the kingdom of God is here — hurrah!

Yet again, even if it were true to say that in *Jesus* God reigned without stint, it was not true that the kingdom had become accepted reality beyond him. He had still to try to express what that rule looked and felt like, he had to call men into that kingdom, he had to impart to them something of his own urgency. And even when they responded and began to catch fire from him, they were still muddle-headed sinners who got so much of it wrong. So it was quickly clear that the final denouement, the lighting-up of the whole cosmos into God's glory wasn't going to happen tomorrow, and if men's freedom, that very air of the kingdom, was to be respected, then the terrible and extraordinary cross was going to have to be part of the road to the kingdom — so there's already a future implied. Startling urgency, pregnant presentness, a long haul ahead — all this seems to be there in the actual life time of Jesus.

The resurrection vindicated Jesus' claims to be God's final declaration of himself, his making of himself fully available to men here and now with no further waiting. The resurrection also confirmed, paradoxically, that the cross was always going to be the way in which his kingdom was going to make its way into men's hearts and lives, and that there could be no short cuts. Yet again, the resurrection demonstrated that Jesus was God's last word, last act to which all else had led up, so that mankind is now living in Act V of the whole drama. And every book of the New Testament is shot through with that expectation that it won't be long now before we see the curtain down and the prizes awarded and Jesus crowned in all men's sight; and this, this generation's expectation, obviously rests on things he himself had said and led them to hope for.

Here we are nineteen hundred and fifty years later. We can agree, maybe, that history *is* different because of what Jesus did — it really is, and no mistake about it — but it isn't obvious that it is nearer to its end than in Jesus' day or than when Wulfstan wrote to the English in the year 999 'This world is in haste and draws nigh to its end!'. What are we to make of all this, what does it mean to be faithful to the New Testament here? What are we trying, if we are, to be faithful to?

It is perhaps worth noting that when the hope of an immediate return of Christ in glory did not materialise — though the fall of Jerusalem and the persecution of the church under Nero all at the same time certainly fanned people's hopes — when the urgent ache began to fade, the church did not collapse. Although II Peter shows a puzzle in men's minds, they do not seem utterly to have been blown off course. It looks as if the *whole* of the church's life and hope was not invested in that expectation.

From the time of the waning of the 'first generation' hope, Christians have tended to follow one of two attitudes. In the main, the Church accepted that it was here to stay in the world for the forseeable future: it developed its structures and theology, it allowed itself to become a strong, respected, feared or despised institution among all the other institutions of the world, it worked out a profound 'timeless' spirituality, but it did keep the words 'And he shall come again' in the creed as a reminder that while *in* the world it was not supposed to be of the world, but looked for a judgement and a hope yet to be revealed; but it included no note of time in the creed, and so the loins girded and lamps lit quality of urgency tended to be lost.

On the other hand, there have always been the protest movements, the Pentecostal outbursts, the Joachim of Floras, the adventist sects who have tried to recapture the spirit of the first days by setting dates as a focus for their breathless faith; and there have been the ascetics who would have no truck with the world, the monks who got up for their night offices in order to be ready at any time for their Lord's return. This kind of faith has always been a challenge to the rest of the faithful, but a somewhat lop-sided challenge, with its falsified predictions, its suspicion of beauty, of marriage, of civilisation as suspect in themselves, rather than as good things standing (at any rate for some) in the way of better things. Yet in spite of its distortion, there remains in this sort of Christianity a reminder of that authentic note of urgency that clearly is there in the New Testament.

If we are to get our heads above water, and try to live by the whole of what is there for us in our tradition, I think we need to aim to hold together three things.

First, the sense of urgency.

Let us be quite clear that when the eternal God, the master of creation and history comes down to earth, that is bound to have a sort of telescoping effect on time itself. The concentration of divine intensity means that the long vistas of human history are bound to be seen as shorter in the light of eternity. Moreover, at least a part of the sense of urgency that we find in the first followers of Jesus arises because he handed on to them nothing less than his own divine ministry — love as I have loved you, be ye therefore perfect as your Father in heaven is perfect, you shall drink the cup that I drink of and be baptised with my baptism, if they have persecuted me they will also persecute you, as the Father hath sent me, even so send I you and so on, and we rightly accept that the holy spirit he breathed upon his disciples was nothing less than his own divine spirit and his own divine commission in them. And all this *does* imply a last lap finality. So that just as Jesus himself in an incredibly short ministry was able to set forth the whole of God's meaning, call out the whole power of evil in opposition and do a perfect work of salvation, all in a more or less predicted time, so the ministry he handed on, if lived to the same perfect pitch of intensity, might indeed have the same effect of telescoping time and changing the whole face of things in an unbelievably short time. Urgency is an authentic note of the gospel because it implies that we are here concerned with nothing less than total divinity now in our human hands. And the only way we know of describing divine urgency in human terms is by setting dates — which invariably turn out to be wrong — but where the mistake does not invalidate the quality it aims to produce.

Secondly, reverence for God's creation.

If you are urgently looking forward to the coming of Christ, and the end of all earthly things as the glory of heaven takes over, you may well be tempted to think of earth as of little worth, to reckon civilisation no more than vain worldly pomp that blinds men to the heavenly reality, to exalt asceticism as the essence of Christianity, to reject the compromise with society that marriage and family life are bound to involve, and to think of the world as a write-off only waiting to be burnt up. Certainly we need ascetics, dedicated celibates, monks and nuns and other austere heroes to remind us that heaven is better than earth and to help us to strain our eyes to descry that far vision. But with this, we shall also need always to recall that heaven and earth are God's creation, made in the mould of Christ himself and waiting for their transfiguration for the manifesting of God's sons. Heaven indeed must be better than earth, but that does not make earth less lovely or generous nor civilisation less valuable, nor the good things of life less thankworthy. When Christians are called to asceticism — apart from the struggle with sin — they are called to give up not what is evil but what is good, for the sake of something better. So along with the gaze, urgently fixed beyond this world on the Christ to be revealed as judge and fulfilment, there will be in authentic Christianity a respect and a care for this world and for human society and for all things good by nature, for streaked through with sin though they all may be, they are to be redeemed by God since they were created by him, and indeed are the stuff out of which the unimaginable glory of heaven is to be made. This is put very well by an old American Christian who said that he was aware that there was still very much coal beneath the earth's surface and he did not think it compatible with the economy of God to see it wasted.

Thirdly, trust and peace.

Side by side with Jesus' very words 'this generation shall not pass away', the New Testament places the words 'but of that hour knoweth no man, neither the angels, nor the son, but the Father only', insisting that the time of the end is not something within the fallible compass of the human imagination, even of Christ's human imagination, but belongs to God alone. Urgency by itself may inject into us a breathless anxiety that the successful achievement of all God's plans depend on *my* faithfulness to his vision and commands. But there are these other texts to remind us that beyond the fallibilities of man, beyond even the splendid faithfulness of man, lies the ultimate responsibility of God who alone knows what the right time means, into whose love we can trustfully hand over all our attempted obedience and all our accepted suffering, and from whom we can receive contentment and peace. So we shall feed on the sacraments of his present victory, and possess our hearts in his peace, trusting that "God reigneth still" and knows what he will make out of all our striving and all his blessing.

I have tried to put together what seem to me to be the essential constituents of a true Christian spiritually rooted in the New Testament and applicable to today, and in doing so I have spoken about history, earth and Heaven.

I began this lecture with history, and in the light of the Christ both behind us and before us, we see that history is neither meaningless nor is it the relentless wheel driving us on in ever increasing anxiety to we know not what. Rather with all the fallibility and freedom of man taken into account, it is a tapestry worked by God, a process that will eventually work the fulfilment of his good and generous plan for the whole. In the middle of what might otherwise be mysterious and unfathomable sequence, he has come himself to show meaning, and in the resurrection demonstrated that the meaning he gives is ultimately victorious over even the worst that can be pitted against it. He has made plain that happiness, fulfilment, significance is not to be found primarily in seeking for my pleasure or in avoiding my censure, but rather in discovering real identity and blessing in going with the grain of his purpose for the whole in Jesus. There will be periods of time — and perhaps the present is one of them when it will be hard to see the thread of purpose running through the life of our nation, the course of our world. Silly optimism is no mark of a serious Christian, but the Christian has seen and known the power of the resurrection, and so he will echo the word the Lord spoke to Lady Julian with reference to the fateful sin of Adam and the greater Amends-making of the cross 'Since I have made well that which is most harm, then it is my will that thou know thereby that I shall make well all that is less'.

We are called to live in two worlds. The eager hopes of heaven showing us how truly to reverence the kingdoms of this world and giving us the energy to long for them to become the kingdom of our God.

As far as our earth and our life on it is concerned, Christian faith bids us receive it gladly at God's hands, reverence it as part of the stuff out of which God's purpose, including God's purpose for us, is made, accept our place within it as instruments of its ultimate redemption, but recall at all times that we hold this high function only as grown up sons of God its creator, sustainer and eternal controller. If I give an example of what I take this to imply, I imagine that every person alive today lives in the awareness that we have, through the exercise of our God-given powers, developed the capabilities either to exhaust the earth's resources or to destroy a large part of the cosmos and those who live in it. No Christian will reflect on these considerations other than with the most deliberate seriousness. But my own instincts make me hesitate to speak too glibly of man's power to destroy God's universe, or to join those who conceive that it will be some rash or wicked act of *man* that will finally bring human history to an end. I believe that with all the power God has given to man it remains God's world, God who does not give his glory to another, and that man's wrong doing, ignorance or folly cannot ultimately bring to nothing what God created good.

Who will be bold enough to speak of heaven where Jesus himself said so little? It is worth insisting that to live with the hope of heaven does not make one less capable of usefulness on earth; rather it frees one from the ties that worldly opinion, worldly reward and worldly censure shackle one with, and enables one to be among the world's most useful servants. But heaven remains a hope and is not yet a vision. It is the hope of limitations removed, of sin no longer a dragging chain, of unbounded imagination blossoming into perfect creativity — and here the medievals managed to sum it up so well in their terse Latin. Augustine, speaking of the transition from 'posse non peccare' to 'non-posse peccare' — from the possibility of not-sinning to 'the inability to sin,' and with Abelard's

Ubi non praevenit
Rem desiderium
Nec desederio
Minus est praemium

not quite so well caught in the English version

Wish and fulfilment
Can severed be ne'er
Nor the thing prayed for
Come short of the prayer.

It is the hope of God finally seen (with that great 'ah'), truly worshipped, loved with powers unabated, and his love overflowing into an unimaginable network of relationships in him. And just as the first coming of Jesus was a true fulfilment of all the ancient promises but could never be foreseen in its wonderfulness, so too, heaven will, we trust, be so utterly natural as to be truly our home, and yet so full of surprise as to preserve us for ever in a state of wonder.

'Eye hath not seen nor ear heard what good things God hath prepared for them that love him.'

Meanwhile, as I began with Jesus Christ as the way in, so I end by directing your eyes to him as the way on.

He stands behind us as God's deed making sense of our history and providing a sure and tested salvation.

He stands ahead of us, the fulfilment of all our wanting.

He stands with us as inexhaustible love and grace; that turns our anxieties into hope again, that gives energy for goodness, and new energy again when we fall on our faces and break our hearts.

That promises that human eyes shall in the end see God and be satisfied.

Beloved, it is a humbling and a heady thing to be welcomed like this by fellow-Christians both of my own and of other churches, by representatives of City and County, by learned academics, by members of other faiths and by a host of Rabbit's friends and relations from every stage of our past life: humbling — to think of you all gathered here to welcome one who inside these robes knows he doesn't add up to that much; heady — because it might give the impression of an importance beyond reality.

So I must not lose my head, but return a very warm thanks to you all, and say at once that I want to respond to you all as a Christian. I want to live here in Bradford as a Christian; I want to encourage those under my care, and maybe others too, to enjoy being Christians, and I should like to commend the Christian faith to any to whom it has not yet happened.

And as I see it, being a Christian is a matter of believing, belonging and behaving.

It's often hard to speak simply and clearly about believing, because in some contexts it's a matter of the mind, in others of the heart, in others of the naked will — and in most contexts it's a mixture of them all.

Yet, although there will doubtless always be some intellectual background to Christian believing, some acceptance of the reasonableness of what is being made of the story about Jesus, for most people faith begins as a tiny, intuitive response somewhere in the heart and the tummy. One is aware of some sort of inner impulse, some urge to pay attention to oneself, maybe the sight of a church overwhelms one with the possibilities that must lie locked up in all that tradition, maybe, clutching at straws, one turns to Jesus to get one out of some fix; and as the inward Yes begins to be formed in the heart, so there appears before one some outward act by which that Yes will be turned into reality of commitment. However it is, it is that actual step of faith that takes one into a trusting relationship with Christ, which one comes to realise is meant to imply a commitment of one's whole life. You may well not foresee what that means or what it will cost — as I certainly did not know where a response I made as a teenager to some words of Alan Cooper, a former Provost of this Cathedral, would eventually land me up— but the initial step of faith opens into a relationship in which God declares more and more of himself, and you discover how much more and more of you there is to be brought under the domination of that relationship.

And I suppose that however much *intellectual* work preceded your step of faith, the entering into the relation of faith is going to require a lot more. It doesn't take long to recognise that the claim you have banked on, that Jesus speaks for God to anyone, in any circumstances and for every bit of his life, is a pretty extraordinary one. Jesus' claims are not exactly self-evident to all, and they may well be dismissed by people who claim that their own experience rules them out of court as either misconceived or unnecessary. So if you want to maintain with honesty that your faith does not fly in the face of reason, and if you want to respond with sympathy and respect to those who can't see why you're so fussed about it, you've got some work ahead of you, digging into the Bible and history and spiritual experience. And I think it is one of the privileges of Christian ministry to be allowed to lead people more deeply into the splendid riches of the Christian tradition, and to show that we do not make the claims for Christ that we do lightly. So let me say a thank you to all the theologians who have taken me deeper into Christian faith — theologians who are, of course, as fallible as psychiatrists or economic advisers — but without whose work Christian believing would be a thinner, less exhilarating, less justifiable thing.

But as you go on, you come to see that faith becomes more and more a question of whether you will really believe in God, will let him be the overriding consideration in actual fact and in every practical situation. Again and again, faced with an intractable problem or an awkward person, the temptation is to rely on the conventional wisdom of the world, or to try to get the better of the other fellow by human cleverness or by playing the authority card, and not to test whether God is really God to be trusted as you say he is.

I don't find faith any easier than any of you, and must

echo the words of the epileptic boy's father in a modern translation: 'Lord, I believe, but not enough.' I shall want to do everything I can to help you to believe in practice what you say you believe, and I shall rely greatly on your faith and love and prayers to help me in my unbelief, so that by enlarging the area of believing, we may give God room to demonstrate his strange Christalmightiness in our midst.

And then, being a Christian is a matter of belonging to Christ with those who are his, and of course there is no way of belonging to Christ except by belonging gladly and irrevocably to all that marvellous and extraordinary ragbag of saints and fatheads who make up the one, holy, catholic and apostolic Church.

For some time now we have got used to being told that people are attracted to Jesus but have no use for the Church, and I think we ourselves have sometimes encouraged this because, knowing from the inside better than anyone else the shameful failings of the Church, we have felt we might somehow dissociate ourselves from them by acquiescing in and even by joining in the world's derision of the Church.

Let us put an end to this.

Let us accept that it is, of course, possible for people to meet Jesus right outside the purlieus of the Church, and perhaps to be reluctant to accept that to go on with Jesus is going to involve getting mixed up with the Church.

Let us accept that since we say we are a community of sinners living only by the grace of a Saviour, we shall have to live with the embarrassment that implies, as also with the miracles again and again it leads on to.

But let us also be reverently proud to be members of Christ's Church, that in the dancing excitement of our common life, people can feel the powerful attraction and welcome of Christ himself. And if that's to be so, then of course we've got to go on and on with this business of working into what the true *life* of the Church really is.

By and large, in most minds the Church is there to conduct services on Sundays whose relation with the rest of life for the rest of the week is less than clear. But if worship is to have awe and glory and compulsion in it, we'll need to know first what sort of a community we are, what we are campaigning for in our daily business, what membership is going to let you in for, what quality of relationships will be required of you — and up-to-God worship as the heart of all that.

One of the most striking pictures of the Church is that given in the first Epistle of St. Peter to bunches of new converts in Asia Minor waiting to be baptised, and being instructed in what their baptism will imply. They are told about their responsibility to *be* the Church, they are told about morals, about political attitudes, about labour relations, about home life, about community life and about their reaction to harassment if it comes. In all this they are shown how to be a community of Christ with his cross as the operative pattern — even hereunto were ye called. They are not told anything about going to church on a Sunday, simply because there were no churches and there were no Sundays either. We are lucky to have both, but it's a good thing every now and then to think churches and Sundays right out of your minds altogether, and then see if your regular workaday community life could be shown to hang together round Christ and the pattern of his cross. Let us aim to close the gap that so easily opens between Jesus and the Church, so that belonging to Jesus and belonging to one another in his Church are seen, in our fermenting creativity, in our purposefulness and in our tested affection for one another, to be the same thing.

And that leads straight on to behaving.

Quite simply, to be a Christian is to belong to a body which behaves as it says it believes. Our corporate and our individual behaving is to say Jesus.

Because our behaving is rooted in our believing and belonging to him, it should be natural, though it's going to take a good deal of fighting ourselves and giving room to his Spirit before it is; it should have a note of confidence and hopefulness in it because it is taking God seriously; it should have generosity, a courteous respect, yet a passion for goodness in any company, arising out of the life we live together hard up against Christ.

And Christian behaving is not so much a private code of personal conduct, though that will be part of it, as something that has to be worked out in relation to the actual circumstances we find we are in, just as leaven finds itself by being put in the dough and salt becomes useful when it's in the cooking. So Christian behaving is activity that tries to give room for Christ to express himself in grace and judgement in every situation.

Now let's be clear. Christ said nothing directly about unevenly distributed unemployment, about nationality bills, about nuclear armaments, about attitudes to technological development, about the rights of women, about comprehensive education, about closed shops. So there's work to be done, listening to the experts, testing what they say against what Jesus did teach that's relevant, and against the whole impact of his person before we come to rough out lines of Christian behaving, and it's not likely that all Christians will arrive at the same answer, certainly not all at once. But part of the whole movement for Christian unity must include, I suppose, some gradual approximation to common lines of action that will express the mind of Christ.

But let us also be clear that there is no pattern of Christian behaving that of itself and automatically says Jesus without our actually naming his name — though there are ways of behaving that automatically cancel out anything we might want to say about him. So Christian behaving will inevitably, and I hope gladly, involve speaking his name and inviting people to look at Jesus and to listen to him, to consider what he offers and what he asks. But that gospel speaking must go with gospel behaving so that one voice of Christ is heard, one picture of him painted and one power of him made available.

I have drawn an ambitious sketch of the Christian life, the sort of life I shall pray this Bradford flock will live, the sort of life I should like to live with them.

Will it be just words?

Well, it could be if I had my way.

But, although I have prayed to speak in his name, beyond and differently from my hopes and anticipations, God has another time-table, key people I haven't yet met, ways of doing things that would not have occurred to me, problems I shall be afraid of but which will turn out to be signposts to ways forward, and it's by recognising God's hand in all this that we may let him fill today's hopes with his reality.

We must today pray that you and I together may be alert and responsive to the living God.

May we continue that way.

An Ordination Charge

I want to entitle this Ordination Charge — 'Shades of the Prison House'. I expect you will recognise the quotation from Wordsworth's 'Ode on the Intimations of Immortality from Recollections of Early Childhood' — to whose romantic notion I have no wish to suggest I in any way subscribe. But the lines 'Shades of the Prison House begin to close upon the growing boy' are telling and I think you will recognise the fear and the danger some of you will already have thought of and which I want to try to speak of tonight.

The basic thesis of this charge is that the Church of God is not divided into two groups, two unequal elements, clergy and laity, but that the People of God is what it says it is, it is all and only laity, and it needs to be glad of it and remember it all the time. Clergy are laity, with a special calling, a special anointing, a special function and they are a special sign that God means redemption for all the world, but they remain laity, and woe betide them if they ever forget it. Shades of the prison-house will close upon them, trying year by year to force them into a clerical mould, but insofar as they allow themselves to be ensnared, they betray their calling, and help the Church to fall under that terrible condemnation of David Edwards, that of all the great religions of the world, the Christian Church is the most heavily clerically dominated. You are laity, and unless, in the midst of all your clerical duties and responsibilities, you preserve a lay heart, in the end you will not have served the Church of God as he calls you to do.

Let me do my best to administer a bit of comfort to your hearts by speaking briefly about the four special things that I think do apply specially to clergy within the whole body of Christ.

First, I spoke of a special calling, and this goes with the first question in the ordination service — do you believe, as far as you know your own heart, that God has called you to the office and work of whatever it is? And the basis of your ministry lies in that calling. As I read the New Testament, all men are called to be Christians, to holiness, to willingness to face suffering, but there is not, as far as I can find, any teaching about Christians being called to be doctors, teachers, butchers, bakers or candle-stick makers. The only specifically defined 'vocation' that I can find is the calling to be full-time servants of God, or what we are now pleased to call clergy. So rejoice in the fact that God has taken special trouble to cast his eye upon you, and to affirm you with a special calling.

Secondly, I spoke of a special anointing. And I have in mind here a special spiritual grace, for God does not call without providing the necessary equipment. There are in the ministerial life great stretches of bare wilderness, patches of dry, waterless waste, periods where all spiritual enthusiasm seems to die, and you think you are gone for good. But, in fact, again and again these eventually, and eventually may be a long time, turn out to be times in which God takes you down to a deeper resource in him than you were ever aware of before. In the meanwhile, you must trust that God keeps special grace for the clergyman in his loneliness, and the reason why you, whatever anyone else may do, must keep yourself in a firm discipline of prayer, is so that you may keep yourself set before the God who is always reaching out trying to feed, bless, inspire, renew and delight you. You have but to read the lives of any of the saints to see that of those from whom God asked most, to them he invariably imparted special grace by which the whole world has been enriched. TRUST — it is promised to you, and look out for it.

Thirdly, I spoke of a special function and this is particularly related to your theological formation. You are required to be competent professionals, getting more and more competent as your experience grows. You are required to know the substance of the Christian faith and be able to show its convincing universality in strong and true fashion. You are required to have worked out the meaning of leadership in a responsible Church, so that you are not just an opportunist, but so that people are helped to see what is God's purpose with the Church, and to see that it is aiming to follow that purpose.

You are required to be competent in Church, so that when people come to Church they are not simply exasperated by the ridiculous triviality and sloppiness of what goes on, but can feel something of themselves being lifted up to God. And you are required to be able to help people learn to pray and develop and grow in prayer when they think they have, in fact, got stuck. We sometimes talk as if the development of a strong ministry of the laity will put the clergy out of a job. This is rubbish. The more we have a fully firing laity, the more professionally competent clergy we shall require, and no other sort will be any use to the Church at all.

And lastly, I said you are a special sign that God means redemption for all the world. I may say a bit more about this later on, but for the moment, what I mean is that clergy ought to look as if they are getting freer day by day, as if they are being more and more redeemed every day, so that others could think they too might be redeemed. Whereas sometimes, when you see clergy together you can almost watch them narrowing, growing meaner, occupying good minds with clerical trivia, arguing about pay, turning themselves into a very second-rate, self-regarding club, who could only persuade other people outside the Church that there lies no hope of release, redemption, enlargement, enrichment from them. It is especially here that you have a responsibility to recall your laity. For if you, of all people, are not being redeemed, why should anyone else think he might be?

I hope I have said enough to make it absolutely clear to you all that I believe there is a deep and essential responsibility on clergy to be first-class clergy, and you can invariably count on my support to help you in any way that will forward that aim.

But now let me return to my starting point, which was that the Church consists only of laity. This has a bearing on the often repeated and overworked phrase that a lot of clergy like to use about themselves that their job is to be enablers of the laity. I wish they really believed it, and I want to see if I can dig in a bit deeper to what this really means. For the essential question is, what is the actual task of the Church and what is your relation to the forwarding of that task?

Two points:

1. The first task of the Church is to *persuade the world*, *the world*, *the world*, that it has been redeemed by the work of Christ. Now have you got anywhere near to believing

that? Do you believe that God has, in fact, redeemed the motor car industry? I have been lying in hospital in recent days and have looked around at my fellow patients and tried to say to myself — 'all these people have been saved and loved and are being blessed by God.' But there simply isn't a smell of it, and I found it took an enormous mental effort just to hold on to this idea. Huge areas of Society, the Army, the Police, International Corporations, political parties, appear to run entirely by their own laws and have no idea that they are part of the kingdoms of this world that God has set his mark on to turn them into the Kingdom of our God and of his Christ. And most of us don't believe it either. We tend to look at all these very secular areas of life and say the only way to be saved and safe, is to escape from all the ambiguities and corruptions of these strange wastes, and try to live somewhat more ecclesiastical lives with some spiritual and moral guidelines to them that can show you how to live before God. And by and large, that is how we do approach these areas of life — we try to get people out of them into a more Church-orientated life. We find it hard to believe that God loves the *world* and has saved the world. We find it hard to think that God actually created all the world of secular activity and has a design for it, intends it to reflect his glory, does not automatically regard it as sinful and simply shot through with evil, for which there is only any hope by some sort of cauterisation or immunisation. The task of the Church and the task of those who are in some sense the leaders of the Church, is to persuade the world that it is, that it has already been, the object of his love, that it has been redeemed by the power of Christ's cross, and that it has the right to know it and benefit by the grace of that redemption. Now which of you really believes that? I ask because it is, in fact, a plain truth and yet one that is almost incredibly hard to believe in any consciously real way.

2. My second point is to ask, who is going to persuade that world that God has so wrought for it in Christ? It is the Church, not the clergy in the first place, but the Church, which is to say the whole laity who actually live in and make up that world. They are the evidence of God's

redemption there, they are those who ought to suggest that God's great work of salvation is gradually overhauling all opposing forces and showing up the glory of God's great design for his world. And you say your task is to enable the laity there. What usually happens? I recently read a most helpful yet utterly heartbreaking book by Mark Gibbs called 'Christians in Secular Power'. It looks at some of those areas of secular life, some of which I have already referred to, at the people who work there, some of whom are and intend to be serious Christians, and it looks at the sort of so-called ministry to which they have been exposed. Now Mark Gibbs has no doubt whatever that Christians in whatever sphere of life they work need to be regularly and committedly involved in worship, and he also has no doubt that they need some kind of exercise set up for them whereby they can immerse themselves more deeply in the theology that will help them to make sense of what they are doing. But what, along with that, they chiefly need is other Christians who really understand what their world is made-up of and will stand alongside them and affirm them in that world, and not try to persuade them out of it into running some part of the ecclesiastical world, raising money for stewardship campaigns or gradually deserting their world for a clergy world. Now you stop and think for a moment of their world — policemen, military leaders, callings which many Christians have an almost instinctive horror of, international businessmen, where the ethical norms pull in every direction and have hardly been worked out; media men, where it is hard to know what you are really talking about when you use the word truth; politicians for whom the identification of real aims is a continual nightmare — take this for a small example: That great Christian, Gladstone, was once defending one of his policies in the House of Commons, and a member of the opposition got up and said — 'Am I not right that the government itself is divided on this issue?' Gladstone at once replied — 'There is no division in the government'. Someone was later heard to say — 'How he can have had the face to reply like that when he had the resignations of four of us in his pocket, I don't know'. What sort of Christian ministry could be designed to help Gladstone to discern infallibly how the claims of truth and the claims of expediency and national confidence were to be balanced?

When you speak of a ministry to enable the laity, can you imagine what a long patient exercise it is sitting beside people and trying to hear from them not what you think ought to be their problems, but what, in fact, they know are the problems that form the ordinary texture of their lives, their moral dilemmas, their opportunities, may be, of advancing the cause of goodness, and so on.

And when I said the Church is only laity and that the clergy are, and must always remember that they are laity, I am arguing that that is the world in which ministry is to be worked out. It can only be worked out by those who belong there, and unless your heart is deeply there, and you remember continually that these are your brothers, your ministry will, in fact, easily be a deforming ministry. The temptation before the clergyman, the shades of the prison-house closing around him, are to persuade him that his world is a safer world, a cleaner world, a world more immediately open to the holy influences of God, a world, therefore, into which he must do his best more and more to draw those to whom he ministers, rather than affirm them and provide for them in their own world.

Now I think you will recognise that, in order to make a particular point, I have tried to paint as difficult and extreme a picture as I possibly could, and I hope you will have tried hard to absorb what I have been getting at.

But let me bring it down to something a bit nearer to what your situation is likely to be and suggest four avenues of approach in a ministry that will really help you to be enablers of the laity in today's world.

First, I was once involved in the setting-up of a small group of deeply converted Christians, consisting of two management consultants, a journalist, a member of the Gas Board and a very articulate wife! One evening they were charged with conducting Evensong in Church and they did this by trying to explain the difficulties they actually faced in trying to be Christians at work, and then the wife led Intercessions for them. I have rarely attended a more electrifyingly alive Evensong. We need more of that kind of group who ask a congregation, most of whom experienced similar problems, to give them real support before God. It takes time to find out how to set up such groups, but will you have it in mind?

Secondly, can I invite you to recognise that this is where the evangelistic frontier is at the present time? We are in the business of trying to preach the Gospel to the world. This is the world and, by and large, the place where the Church, the laity, the people of God touches the world is at the frontier of secular work. This is where we have to pitch the Gospel, the real Gospel, not of censorship, grunts and gloom, but of blessing, grace, goodwill, hope and salvation.

This means thirdly, particularly as far as clergy are concerned, that your special ministry is to be a theologian in that world. You must listen to what those who live there tell you about its make-up, and not imagine you know all about it and are competent to deliver them moral lectures straight off the reel, but as you listen you have so got to know the Bible and the contents of essential Christian doctrine that you find you are able to ask the sort of questions that release the elements in the situation that point to Gospel. You have got to have the heart of the lay person in the situation, but you must be so increasingly profound Christian theologians that your questions help them to discern how they can lay hold of Christ's blessing and grace which he is constantly longing to stretch out to them.

And let me end by repeating something I said earlier on. A Christian is someone who is redeemed and who, therefore, year by year looks as if he is growing freer, less shackled by bonds of convention and formality. Your own increasing and infectious redeemedness ought to give hope to your flock in spite of all the difficulties that beset them. That redemption is theirs for the having — sometimes terribly hard to lay hold of, sometimes given in moments of simple, blessed grace, but their birthright in Christ, who came and lived and died for them.

Pray God to give you grace that the shades of the prison-house will not close around you, for if they close around you it will be hard for the world to whom you minister to believe that there is redemption and glory for them.

A Christmas Sermon

At Christmas time, the theologians talk about the great christological issues this birth raises, while popular feeling goes for the picturesque details — the oxen by the manger, the wise men on their camels, the baby in the straw.

In the Prayer Book, as far as Christmas Communion was concerned, it looks as if the theologians had it: the Epistle from Hebrews 1 was the great affirmation of the absolute pre-eminence of the Son, and the Gospel from John 1 was the solemn statement of the incarnation of the eternal Word. The Alternative Service Book here offers a number of choices, but it puts the Christmas *stories* from St. Luke before the theological statement from St. John. Do you find that significant or not, a good move or not?

What do the theologians want us to dwell on as we try to come near to the heart of Christmas? Well, two things, mainly —

First, they want us to come to terms with the claim that this baby was born of a virgin mother.

Now, it is a curious thing that if you consider the scriptural accounts without prejudice, the historical evidence for the Virgin birth is much stronger than it is sometimes thought to be. One can think of no reason that will stand up to serious examination why the writers should have wanted to fabricate the story, and indeed, I suppose the only reason why the story is questioned is that virgin births are hardly common and so not easy to swallow, but if, on other grounds, this birth is unique, that's not much of a reason. So it seems to me not at all unreasonable to take the evangelist's assertion at face value. BUT, oddly enough, neither they nor any of the other New Testament writers seem at all concerned to lay any theological emphasis on the matter. Perhaps we ought to take our cue from them, and not rush too quickly into asserting what the Virgin Birth 'means', or into anathematising those who have difficulty with it; but since it can hardly be without significance, it has commonly been taken to mean, in J. S. Whale's words, that 'he came into history, he did not simply come out of it'.

And whether that's a proper inference to draw or not, it

leads us straight into the second of the theologians' concerns — the question of the incarnation of God's Son. And here again, we are faced with an unparalleled and so paradoxical notion. We used to be content with those marvellous old paradoxes:

> O wonder of wonders, which none can unfold,
> The Ancient of Days is an hour or two old;
> The Maker of all things is made of the earth,
> Man is worshipped by angels, and God comes to birth.

But these days, for the entirely praiseworthy reason that we have laid more stress on the total reality of Christ's manhood, we have not been content to rest in paradox, and have tried to see if we can dispense with the notion of incarnation, the notion of God the Eternal Son coming to be conceived in the Virgin's womb, and have been searching for some explanation easier to compass with our imaginations and to put together with our minds. And so serious thinkers, some of whom contributed to 'The Myth of God Incarnate' and others who would never have thought of doing any such thing, have tried to see if we can think of Jesus as in every genetic respect strictly a man and no more, with no secret ingredient added that the rest of us do not have, yet a man so totally given to God and so transparent to God that in this *man* we meet God as we meet him in no other person in history.

Now any serious Christian will know that it is a good thing to try to get inside these modern christologies, because we ought not simply to rest in paradoxes if they can be resolved, but it seems to me that they fail to explain one vital thing. Why is it that Jesus of Nazareth was given to God and open to God as no other person in history has ever been? Why is it that, whereas the rest of us have to be converted in order to pray and even then so often find it hard grind, for Jesus it seems to have been the natural breath of his life from the beginning — 'Did you not know that I must be about my Father's business?', says the boy of twelve. Why is it that all the world's other holy men seem to have stumbled their way into the path of God's service, needing to admit and repent of faults or misunderstandings of God's will, whereas Jesus seems to have been able to give all his talents in one integrated dedication to God from the outset of his ministry, never straying a foot to the right or left from the way of his Father's will, with never a word of regret or contrition or apology on his lips, never a second thought because he had got it wrong first time. Progress and development there undoubtedly were — he learned obedience through the things that he suffered, says the Epistle to the Hebrews — yet there are no false steps, no clouds of depression, no agonising self-criticism, no incidents or periods of which we could say 'Well, he wasn't reflecting God very well there'. Why is this man's manhood so undeviatingly directed towards God? Jesus is without question like us as a man, but he is not like any one of us. It is that uniqueness, even of his manhood, that is not explained except by some such doctrine as incarnation: this man somehow *was* God; this virgin-born baby can be none other than God's inexplicable gift to us of himself.

But while the theologians are struggling without falsehood and without omission to get facts and explanation to fit together into one satisfactory whole for the devout *mind*, the designers of Christmas cards, the television producers, the Sunday School teachers, the artists and the poets — all the communicators, that is — are concentrating on and letting the imagination run free with the marvellous Christmas *stories*, with all those extra, beautiful, legendary details added, the silence of the night, the oxen kneeling at midnight, the shepherds' conversation on the hillside, the journey of the Magi, now crowned kings and bearing solemn names — and sometimes even managing to get Father Christmas rolled in as well. They are not going for our minds so much as for our imaginations and our hearts, to lead us above all to be moved in our feelings to open our hearts to this baby. It is perhaps the danger of a faith like ours that because the heart of it is a story, so it risks being rounded out with legends that before long have become tradition not to be questioned. But it remains true that it is the story that takes us to the heart of the matter; it is in the story of this wondrous birth that our hearts and emotions are stirred and touched. And if Bishop Stephen Neill is right when he says that the function of the emotions is to move the will, that's where our wills to worship and to follow are activated.

So are we to go for the theologians' questions and explanations or for the communicators' stories?

We must go for both.

To concentrate solely on the profound theological significance of the birth at Christmas might suggest that first-class Christianity is only for the intellectual, and would isolate us from all those popular but sincere movements of the heart that are real, if only preliminary, responses to God's generosity in giving us his Son.

To concentrate solely on the story is to relegate Christianity to sentimentality, is to rate ourselves a feebler generation than many of our forefathers who were prepared to wrestle with questions of truth, is to finish up with a Christmas card folk religion. The miraculous story needs to be tested for truth and meaning.

And I think this tension between the mind and the emotions, which is perhaps felt most strongly in our response to the event of Christmas, speaks of something quite fundamental about the way in which we should be Christians. Let me make two brief points.

First, Christians are those who contend for truth and will not be satisfied with less than the truth, who will not be afraid to put question-marks against revered tradition in their search for truth, who will probably need from time to time to tumble over into heresy in their desire not to fudge the evidence, and who, in it all, will be developing a transparent quality of trustworthy truthfulness that goes right to the heart of them. But *the* Truth himself was a little child feeding at his mother's breast, and stretching out a tiny hand to the animals and depending on others for everything. And that quality surely ought to be in us too in our defence of the truth, the quality of the little child which Christ esteemed so highly, the gentleness, the winningness, the willingness to need even those one does not succeed in persuading. Christians in controversy need to learn these two responses. I once watched Mrs. Whitehouse in argument with four theologians on television, and it was obvious from the outset that none of them liked her line. But one alone — and I'm glad to say he is a friend — one alone was courteous to her and treated her as a lady, and that was the most impressive thing about the interview. And many of you must have seen that famous interview between Archbishop Antony Bloom and Marghanita Laski, when the Archbishop moved that fairly tough agnostic to a sudden humility by the gentle respect with which he treated her. Christmas bids us get the impossible mix right, to be fearless contenders for ungarbled truth for the mind, yet with gentleness for the heart, to give a reason for the hope that is in us, but with meekness and fear.

The other point is about Christian preaching, and perhaps here the emphasis is the other way round. Christian preaching aims at the heart, because it is there that decisions are made. And Anglicans are often poor evangelistic preachers — and I should include myself here — because we are a bit reluctant to speak to the heart. Do you remember Dr. Johnson's remark to a young man who asked, 'Are not So-and-So's sermons addressed to the passions?' 'They are nothing, Sir', the Doctor replied, 'be they addressed to what they may' — a fair comment on a lot of Anglican preaching. It is true that the whole non-directive emphasis of today warns us that we must treat other people's deciding mechanisms with the tenderest respect and never use unfair means to force them to decisions not truly their own. But there will be occasions when we fail to respect people just by not putting the question, just by failing to say, 'You will sell yourself to dithering mediocrity for life if you fail to recognise that a decision here is crucial'. But in speaking straight to the heart when it is right to do so, we must be sure in our minds that we are not asking a man to commit himself to something that later will turn out to affront his reason, and we should be ready to state our grounds when challenged. It is the evangelist par excellence who must aim for intellectual integrity, so that in longing to be a vehicle of God's Spirit to men's hearts, he may not narrow but rather enlarge their minds and indeed set their feet in a larger and larger room of truth.

I think I need say no more.

The old Christmas Bidding Prayer invited us in heart and mind to go even unto Bethlehem and see this thing which is come to pass *and* the Babe lying in a manger.

It's good to recall the background to the Epistle to the Colossians, from which the title of this sermon comes.

The Colossians evidently didn't think that turning to Christ had made an absolute difference to their lives. They accepted that Christ had altered the religious centre of things for them, but there were other powers in the universe who had to be placated, powers that determined their fate and their worldly circumstances, which you couldn't afford to overlook.

Paul says two astonishing things in the Epistle to the Colossians. He does not deny that there may be other powers in the universe, but he says first that whatever powers there are in heaven or on earth were created through Christ and for Christ. Christ and Christ alone is the original mould of all God's creation, and there are no other creative powers apart from Christ. Secondly he says that at the cross Christ overcame the combined efforts of all the powers to defeat him, and displayed them like conquered captives in his victory train. Lord of all by creation; Supreme victor by the cross. And if you think of the powers as such things as your psychological inheritance, your racial disposition, the limitations of your political circumstances, the climate of what is believable into which you are born, that is a pretty astounding claim. So Paul is saying to the Colossians, so far from having to placate any other powers, by your baptism into Christ you have died to all past allegiances, you now have one Lord only, and risen with Christ you belong essentially to the one and only victorious Lord, whose hand is over all your circumstances. You have died — your life as Christians, your whole life, is lived in association with the risen Christ. With that as background, let us notice some of the things Paul says about being risen with Christ.

First, seek those things that are above — set your mind on things that are above, not on things that are on the earth.

I think that can sound a bit misleading. It could suggest that Christians are essentially head-in-the-air, unpractical people, good at discussing abstract ideas but no good at mending bicycles or unable to give sensible advice to engaged couples. If you read St. Paul's other letters, you can see that he cannot mean that. 'Things that are on the earth' must mean all the care and anxieties that made the Colossians feel they had to placate other powers. And 'seeking the things that are above' must mean always keeping the risen Christ and the truth of his victory as the reality before your eyes. We are to live as if the resurrection determines the confidence with which we go at the whole of life.

Then, your life is hid with Christ in God. Why hid? Well, I suppose because the truth of the resurrection, in spite of clues dotted about all around us and all over history, is not self-evident. I suppose our lives are intended to manifest the truth of Christ's resurrection, just as Christ's resurrection undergirds our lives.

Paul then goes on to argue that the risen life is demonstrated in a new quality of moral living. If you died to the things of the earth, then you must accept as *essentially dead and done with* the moral dispositions of the old life, sins of the flesh, greed, envy, quarrelsomeness, dishonesty. I don't think this is just a psychological couéism, pretending that defects in your conduct don't really exist. I think it is essentially prayer — it is saying to God: 'I accept before you that faults and failings in me belong essentially to my old unredeemed life and can't stand up before you. Will you please live your risen life in me, and will you enlighten me so that I open more and more of myself to your grace, and let your redemption overcome my dead-self and work to change me.' And if we follow the advice Paul gives to the Galatians, this is more likely to happen as we expose ourselves to other Christians in the fellowship of the Holy Spirit, rather than just by aiming at individual self-improvement by strict, private self-examination.

And that leads me to what seems to me the most striking feature of this passage, the place where Paul says, 'you have put off the old nature . . . and have put on a new nature which is being renewed in knowledge after the image of its creator: here, there cannot be Greek and Jew, circumcised and uncircumcised, barbarian, Cythian, slave, free man, but Christ is all and in all.'

Let us think for a bit on this astonishing statement. It means first, that the new man into whom we are incorporated by our baptism in the risen Christ, is essentially a new civilisation. God made the old covenant with the race of the Jews and it was held together by ties of blood, so that Jews the world over have a common loyalty to one another, are aware of belonging to a chosen race, will support one another and have been preserved as a distinct and recognisable people against the most terrible odds. The new covenant in Christ's blood makes Christians of all races blood relations of Christ and so, blood relations with one another. What Paul is claiming here is that Christians are a new race, and, what is more, are a pointer to what God had originally in mind when he created mankind. Christians, a new race, putting their loyalty to their blood relationship in Christ above every other, what we might call more natural, physical loyalties to family, nationality, colour. Is that what being a Christian means to you?

Risen with Christ on this showing means: Belonging to a redeemed race which, without despising other ties, takes priority over them all: Belonging to a new civilisation which offers the whole world some glimpse of what God intended and intends to mean by mankind.

Secondly, Paul says that in the new risen mankind, all that divided the old mankind is left behind, and it is not too easy to imagine oneself into what he actually means. Here he speaks of the religious divisions between Jew and Gentile; the cultural divisions between educated and uneducated; the social divisions between slave and free, and in the parallel verse in Galatians he adds the sexual difference between male and female. And it is this last which requires that we think carefully about what he means, because he obviously can't mean that when we turn to Christ we cease to be men and women and suddenly all find ourselves members of the Middlesex Regiment. And equally, it can't mean that differences of race, culture and taste are of no significance, or that the new civilisation is a coffee-coloured amalgam, enjoying stereotyped light music and moderate literature, with no experts, no specialists, none of those differences that give richness to human exchange.

So what does it mean?

It may help first to glance at the final phrase, 'But Christ is all and in all'. In the early part of the Epistle to the Colossians, Paul has not only claimed that Christ is the original mould of all God's creation, but says he is also the goal to which all things move; he is the means by which all things are reconciled into one. Christians as far apart as Ireneaus in the second century and Teilhard de Chardin in ours, have been fascinated by this idea of the gathering up of all things in Christ. In the light of this notion, the differences we see before us with a bitterness and contempt that we have come to think indispensable from them, are not the last word on the subject. Christ intends to harmonize them into a pattern in himself, and we need to keep our sights set there. Moreover, Christ has found no difficulty in entering into the experience of every kind of person however much they are separated by human convention. And if that is so, then they are already tending towards their ultimate fulfilment and redemption in Christ.

So if we turn back to the differences that Paul says are overcome in the new mankind, I take it that it is the divisions, the divisiveness, the bitterness, the contempt, that have so long gone with the differences that are to be left behind, and when that is gone, we may see better how the actual differences are meant to resolve themselves.

If I take the hardest of the examples, not in our Epistle, but in Galatians — 'neither male nor female': as no-one wants to see our sexual differences erased, least of all Christians, who thank God for the goodness of his creation. But we know well enough that over centuries man has built into the difference a sense of patronising superiority which does not take seriously that Christ can be found in women as well as men. And what essentially, it seems to me, Women's Lib. is about, is that women are saying they see no reason why their role should be determined for them by men, why men's opinions of this and that should always carry the casting vote. And in this, if Paul's argument is sound, every Christian must agree with them. Once the attitude is changed, then what is to be made of the differences can be apprehended in quite a new way. To take a trivial example which I don't want to make anything of, I once asked a shy little girl what the Church ought to do about the Ordination of women: she replied, 'Why don't you ask the girls, you can trust them can't you?' I do not offer that as a practical piece of advice, because I don't know how to ask the girls, but surely that girl had got the utterly right approach. She took it for granted that, in Christ, men and women, though different, are equal, equally deserving of each other's respect and trust. Start there, and what is to be made of our inherited differences can gradually come to light and take us on to the richness Paul was looking to in the ultimate Christianity.

So, this Easter invitation to be risen with Christ turns out, on examination, to be a much larger thing than might have been foreseen.

What does it require us practically to do? First, it requires that all our spiritual attention be concentrated on the risen Christ, that we focus on him in our prayers, that we let God expound his significance for us, that we trust him as the beginning and the end of all God's intentions.

Secondly, it requires that we trust the risen Christ dwelling within us to be the strength of all our moral development. I don't think this means that year by year we shall be able to be more satisfied with ourselves and our prayers, though we shall certainly take seriously the evidently offensive things in us. The test of growth is likely to be that while not losing sight of moral rectitude, we find ourselves able to make more and more room in ourselves for other people, even the most scandalous or infuriating.

Thirdly, it requires that we try to draw closer to one another, and through Christ, to begin to feel in ourselves the consciousness of being the seeds of the new mankind: obviously, this will affect the way we feel about international relations, about political priorities, about the aims of education and all those dark corners where our unredeemed instincts are in favour of preserving separation.

But chiefly, being risen with Christ means having an intense, a large view of Christ, and letting his victory be the dominating factor in all our praying, thinking, hoping, trusting, until it is plain to all that we are the Easter people, looking forward to the day when our lives are no longer hid with Christ, but revealed in Christ.